Writing
for Industry
An Instruction Manual

Anita J. Lehman
College of San Mateo

Holt, Rinehart and Winston
New York   Chicago   San Francisco   Philadelphia
Montreal   Toronto   London   Sydney
Tokyo   Mexico City   Rio de Janeiro   Madrid

Library of Congress Cataloging in Publication Data

Lehman, Anita J.
  Writing for industry.

  Includes index.
  1. Technical writing.   I. Title.
T11.L46   1984   808'.0666   83-10741

AL

ISBN 0-03-061963-7

CBS COLLEGE PUBLISHING
Holt, Rinehart and Winston
The Dryden Press
Saunders College Publishing

Preface

To the instructor

Writing for Industry: An Instruction Manual is a practical and simple approach to technical writing. It is designed for a lay (uninitiated) audience with a wide range of specialties.

In command form, *Writing for Industry* gives clear, easy-to-follow instructions for different types of technical communication, from mechanism descriptions to detailed formal reports. The manual is designed as a workbook with examples and exercises.

The text is laid out as a formal technical report and is divided into four parts: Part One, Communication (theory and importance); Part Two, Information Retrieval; Part Three, Learning to Write; and Part Four, Technical Writing Stylebook. Appendixes include Looking for a Job (Job Investigation, Letter of Application, and a Résumé); Sample Student Papers; and Writing Guides and Checklist of Corrections. The book concludes with a Glossary.

Each part includes a statement of performance objectives, step-by-step instructions followed by models, a summary, and accompanying exercises.

To the student

Writing for Industry: An Instruction Manual is designed to help you understand the importance of communication in business and in industry and to give you a sense of achievement.

The manual is designed to give you simple instructions for finding information in the library and recording and storing it, writing different types of technical communication, setting up a job search strategy, and writing letters of application and résumés. The manual concludes with Sample Student Papers, Writing Guides and Checklist of Corrections, and a Glossary.

You will learn how to write clear, concise, and forceful prose; and in simple lay language you will learn how to think logically by using *deductive logic* (to tell where you are going, to go there, and to tell where you have been).

You will increase your opportunities for promotion on the job because communication skills in business and industry are as much a necessity as are technical skills.

Contents

PART ONE **Communication**   1

PART TWO **Information Retrieval**   11

List of Figures and Tables

Goals

PART ONE

1.0 Effecting Attitude Change

1.0.1 Importance of Communication

The primary goal of Part One is to determine the importance of communication skills for upward job mobility. Writing skills are as important as technical skills for career advancement, as sufficient evidence shows.

1.0.2 Meaning of Communication

The second goal of Part One is to show technical writing as a process that links communication systems in industry and reports practical information to a specific audience.

1.0.3 Words and Symbols

Third, Part One stresses the necessity of fitting words and symbols into the audience's frame of reference. If the audience does not understand the meaning of the words and symbols, the message does not get through.

1.0.4 How Communication Works

Fourth, Part One demonstrates how information travels from source to destination: sender to receiver, writer to audience.

1.0.5 How to Communicate

Last, Part One asserts the importance of anticipating the audience's needs so there is no breakdown in communication. It describes levels of language and kinds of definitions to use for specific audiences, and emphasizes the importance of eliminating all barriers to communication (NOISE#?*!): misspelling, jargon, overwriting, incorrect punctuation.

PART TWO

2.0 Learning Key Techniques of Information Retrieval

2.0.1 Importance of Information Retrieval

The purpose of Part Two is to help you save time and write good reports based on good research.

Part Two will help you learn your way around the library; know where to find material; know how to record, store, and document data.

2.0.2 Using the Access Tools in the Library

Part Two will help you learn to use the *access tools* for the general book collection, reference book collection, technical journals and newspapers, audio-visual collection, on-line databases, microfiche, and computer call-up systems.

Once you have learned how to use these *access tools,* you will understand the amazing amount of data available in the library.

2.0.3 How to Store Data

Once you have learned how to find the data, you will learn how to take notes and record your sources for documentation. Careful note-taking will systematize your research and save you time and effort.

2.0.4 How to Document Data

To complete your research strategy, Part Two will give you a simple method of footnoting data and recording sources in a bibliography at the end of your report.

PART THREE

3.0 Learning to Write

3.0.1 Importance of Learning to Write

The major goal of Part Three is to help you learn to write at a level of competence for upward job mobility.

3.0.2 How to Be Clear, Concise, and Forceful

Part Three will help you present, in clear, concise, and forceful written prose, findings encountered on the job: mechanism descriptions, process descriptions, instructions, memorandums, informal reports, formal reports, and correspondence.

3.0.3 How to Use the Language of Graphics and Textual Delineators

Part Three will show you how to use the language of graphics (tables and figures) to enhance your written material, to make your writing clear and forceful. And you will learn the value of textual delineators and numbering that serve as organizational guides and transitional devices:

1. Captions
2. Headings
3. Subheadings
4. Listings
5. Numbering

PART FOUR

4.0 Technical Writing Stylebook

4.0.1 Purpose of Writing Stylebook

The purpose of the technical writing stylebook is to provide a guide for easy reference.

You will learn some basic English grammar written in simple, easy-to-understand language designed for an audience unfamiliar with formal, technical grammar.

4.0.2 Content of Writing Stylebook

The technical writing stylebook is alphabetized for handy reference. In command form, you will learn simple instructions for abbreviations used in industry, capitalization, correct usage, the exact word and the simple word, correct pronouns, numerals, parallel structure, punctuation, spelling, verb forms, and correct vocabulary.

APPENDIXES

The Appendixes include the following helpful materials:

Appendix A   Looking for a Job: Investigation, Letter of Application, and a Résumé
Appendix B   Sample Student Papers
Appendix C   Writing Guides and Checklist of Corrections

GLOSSARY

Writing
for Industry

An Instruction Manual

PART ONE
Communication

Where You Are Going

In Part One you are going to learn

- the importance of communication skills for upward job mobility
- the kinds of communication you will encounter on the job
- the meaning of communication
- words and symbols
- how to communicate to a specific audience

1.0.1   The Importance of Communication

In industry you will spend a part of each day in some form of communication. You must, therefore, understand how the communication process works, how to analyze your audience, and how to make certain there is no breakdown in communication. For upward mobility in industry, communication skills are as much a necessity as are technical skills.

As a beginning technician, you will probably not be called on to do any formal technical report writing. However, you will probably be required to write instructions to the technician on the next shift who will want to know what you have completed and what he or she is expected to do.

You may want to write a memorandum or a short informal report to your supervisor suggesting a change or an improvement in a process or a mechanism in your department. You may be called on to write a progress report on a job, a periodic report (weekly or monthly), or a travel report.

Technicians who are skilled in their jobs also need communication skills if they want to advance.

Jodi Mantooth, a personnel administrator at Signetics, says, "I started as a trainee on the swing shift at a salary lower than that of the janitor, but I had a *plan*. And now six years later I am in management and I am still moving up. I learned everything I could about communication skills, and that has made the difference."

Jim Lisec, personnel representative at United Airlines, says, "A good part of my job is counseling employees how to get ahead.

"To be chosen as a supervisor, an employee has to be able to tell others what to do. The biggest lack on the job is communication skills. A technician can make great widgets; but if he can't communicate what he is doing or how to do it, he is worthless. The person who can effectively sell himself goes up the fastest. So allow flexibility for many career paths. A good foundation in communication skills is extremely valuable."

Steven Lloyd, manager of the Piping Department at McKee Company, states that all employees have to be technically excellent, but to go up the promotional ladder requires ability to communicate in writing.

"For example," Lloyd says, "there are up to 5,000 IOC's (interoffice communications) written on one job from office to field, from field to office, from office to office, field to field."

Lloyd adds that even at the beginning level, design time is wasted that could be costly. Technical things are all done in writing, so the ability to put things down clearly is paramount.

And, finally, Anne Ebell, electronics engineer at Intel Corporation, says, "Being an engineer is not just being able to sit at a drawing board. The ability to communicate in a number of ways goes into the job."

Technical writing takes many forms: mechanism descriptions, instructions, memorandums, informal reports, and formal reports. If communication is the goal and the audience is kept in mind, then good writing is good writing. Only the format is different.

The model reports in this text may not correspond to your major technical field, or they may not be exactly like the formats used on your job; but they demonstrate well-organized, well-written types of technical communication.

The least that is expected of you in industry is that you are technically qualified. The added dimension to your skills is the ability to communicate. It will make all the difference in your upward job mobility.

1.0.2 The Meaning of Communication

Communication is the act of transmitting information, attitudes, and ideas from one person to another.

The transfer of meaning is always involved. The word *communication* comes from the Latin word *communis,* which means "commonness." When people communicate with one another, they speak the same language; they understand the same technical language.

Technical writing is a process that links a communications system — within the office, office to field, field to office, office to client, client to office — and reports practical information.

The purpose of technical writing is to inform a specific audience of facts and figures, descriptions of mechanisms and processes, instructions, solutions to problems, conclusions, and/or recommendations based on studies.

1.0.3 Words and Symbols

Words and symbols have no meaning on their own. They represent meaning. Words and symbols are merely tools to express ideas.

Therefore, you must make certain that you direct your communication to an audience who will understand your message.

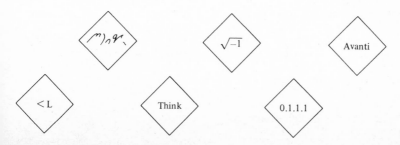

1.0.4 How Communication Works

- First you, the source, receive a stimulus; for example, a dangerous situation has arisen. You have been informed that there is a safety problem in the maintenance division which should be reported to the supervisor.
- Reacting to the stimulus, you form a message (from many possibilities) to an intended audience for a specific purpose.

  There is a potential safety problem in the wing connection, and I am working to correct it.

- Then you *encode* the message (express it in a form that can be transmitted: the spoken word, a written memorandum, a graph, a chart, a picture). You must be sure that you formulate the message accurately and clearly so there is no breakdown in communication. (See Figure 1.1 showing the encoded message.)

MEMORANDUM

DATE: 14 April 198_

TO: Lou DeFreitas, Supervisor
FROM: Kenny Childs
SUBJECT: Safety Problem

I am working to correct a potential safety problem in the wing connection. The joint showed weakness under stress.

We are testing replacement pieces, and with the delivery of stronger steel from Westinghouse the $\frac{3}{8}$-inch-thick test piece container is half full.

I have devised a method for cutting bevels on the $\frac{3}{8}$-inch material that will speed up the process. By using a spacer of the right width, we can properly and quickly position a piece for beveling. We will take only a short period of time to cut the pieces needed to replace the present wing connection.

Please let me know if you foresee any problems. I think the work we are doing to correct the safety problem in the wing connection will do the job.

FIGURE 1.1 Encoded Message

- The receiver *decodes* the message within his or her experience and knowledge. The receiver of the memorandum, the supervisor in the same department, shares the experience and knowledge of the sender. (See Figure 1.2.)

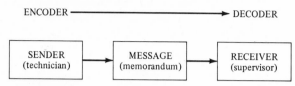

FIGURE 1.2 How Communication Works

1.0.5   How to Communicate

Now that you understand how information travels from source to destination, you know that technical communication is directed to a specific audience: a technical audience, a lay audience, or a combination of both.

• Plan a Strategy to Make Your Audience Understand.

The levels of language and kinds of definitions will always depend on the audience. A technical audience will understand your words and symbols, so you will not have to define specific terms for them.

However, a lay audience may not be able to decipher your message, so you will have to define your terms to make certain your audience fits into your frame of reference.

The simplest way to define terms for lay audiences is to use analogies, familiar comparisons they can understand.

For example, an ellipse is like an egg. It is oval in shape.

Parallel lines are like railroad tracks. They never meet.

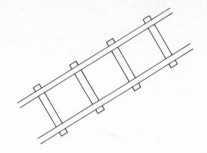

• **Eliminate All Barriers to Communication (Noise !@#$%¢&).**

Every time you misspell a word, use jargon, punctuate incorrectly, or overwrite, you interrupt your message. Study the following examples and note the clarity of the corrected messages.

1. Misspelling

   Their is a ninty-nine percent chance of a noticable problem.

   Noise eliminated:

   There is a ninety-nine percent chance of a noticeable problem.

2. Jargon

   An inoperative criteria analysis will be finalized.

   Noise eliminated:

   The malfunction is being studied, and the report will be finished soon.

3. Incorrect punctuation

   Jame's theory does not hold up, therefore we have to substitute our's.

   Noise eliminated:

   James's theory does not hold up; therefore we have to substitute ours.

4. Overwriting

   The company must obviate any misuse of its funds by delineating strict guidelines.

Noise eliminated:

The company must prevent any misuse of its funds by drawing strict guidelines.

Where You Have Been

Communication skills are as important as technical skills for career advancement.

When you communicate, you must keep your audience in mind and make certain that your audience understands your message. Plan your strategy so that you fit into your reader's *frame of reference.*

Personality is your effect on other people. Every time you write, your personality shows.

Take pride in your work. Eliminate all barriers to communication that create noise for your reader.

Exercises

1. Interview a technician in your major field and ask how much time he or she spends writing and on what kinds of writing.

2. Interview a person in management in an industry related to your major field and ask him or her how much importance communication skills have played in his or her career.

3. What is a *lay audience?* Describe one in your field.

4. What is a *technical audience?* Describe one in your field.

_____

_____

_____

_____

_____

_____

5. In a brief essay describe the kind of audience you (your fellow students) are and why.

_____

_____

_____

_____

_____

_____

_____

6. How do you define terms for a lay audience?

_____

_____

7. Find an article in a technical journal in your field, one that is written for a technical audience, and rewrite it into a popular article for a lay audience.

8. What are some of the barriers to communication that cause noise?

_____

_____

_____

_____

_____

_____

9. Translate the following jargon into clear, concise, and forceful language.

   Data developed and examined during the course of this project as defined in the authorizing documents suggest that the system under study will, within specified parameters, perform as predicted.

   _____

   _____

   _____

   _____

   We solicit any recommendations that you wish to make, and you may be assured that any such recommendations will be given our careful consideration.

   _____

   _____

   _____

   _____

10. What are your strengths in communication?

    _____

    _____

    _____

    _____

    _____

11. What are your weaknesses in communication?

    _____

    _____

    _____

    _____

    _____

12. How much of a commitment are you willing to make to overcome these weaknesses?

_____

_____

_____

_____

13. How do you see yourself ten years from now? Inside or outside? Standing up or sitting down? What part will communication skills play in this picture? Why? Write a brief essay answering these questions.

_____

_____

_____

_____

_____

_____

_____

_____

_____

_____

_____

_____

_____

_____

_____

_____

_____

_____

PART TWO
Information Retrieval

Where You Are Going

In Part Two you are going to learn how to

- gather data
- interpret data   in order to provide a research
- store data   strategy
- document data

2.0.1 The Importance of Information Retrieval

Since time is money in industry, it is important that you develop a research strategy to retrieve, interpret, store, and document information.

In Part Two you will learn your way around the library so that it will be easier to find materials. You will learn how to use the *access tools* for the general book collection, the reference book collection, the technical journals and newspapers, the audio-visual collection, on-line databases, microfiche, and computer call-up systems.

When you have finished, you will have a research strategy that will save you time and, therefore, money.

2.0.2 Use the Access Tools in the Library.

Learn to use the access tools in the library. They are your keys to published information and literature in your field.

Sir Francis Bacon, in the sixteenth century, was able to say, truthfully, that he knew everything there was to know. Today there is so much information that it is impossible to know everything about your own specialty. What *is* important is to know how to find published information when you need it.

General book collection
  Access tool: Card catalog
Reference book collection
  Access tool: Card catalog
    Reference desk
Magazines and newspapers
  Access tool: Indexes
Audio-visual (A-V) collection
  Access tool: Card catalog
    A-V catalog
    Special in-house files
On-line databases
  Access tool: Card catalog
    Reference desk
Microfiche
  Access tool: Card catalog
    Reference desk
Computer call-up system
  Access tool: Reference desk

• Learn to Use the Card Catalog.

Learn to use the card catalog in your library. The cards are filed alphabetically under three entries: author's (or editor's) name, title, and subject. (See Figures 2.1, 2.2, and 2.3.)

```
Ref
TA
151        Eshbach, Ovid Wallace, 1893-1958, ed.
             Handbook of engineering fundamentals,
           prepared by a staff of specialists under
           the editorship of Mott Souders and Ovid
           W. Eshbach.  3d ed.
           New York, Wiley [c1975]
               x, 1530 p. illus. 22cm.  (Wiley
           engineering handbook series)

               Includes index.

                 1.Engineering--Handbooks, manuals,
           etc.  I.Sounders, Mott, 1904- ed. II.
           Title.
  TA151.E8 1974
  ISBN 0-471-24553-4                      620'.002'02
                                              74-7467
                           000 018        LC-MARC
                                                     3
```

FIGURE 2.1 Card Using Author's Name

```
         Handbook of engineering fundamentals
  Ref
  TA
  151    Eshbach, Ovid Wallace, 1893-1958, ed.
  E8        Handbook of engineering fundamentals,
         prepared by a staff of specialists under
         the editorship of Mott Souders and Ovid W.
         Eshbach.  3d ed.
         New York, Wiley [c1975]
             x, 1530 p. illus. 22 cm.  (Wiley
         engineering handbook series)
             Includes index.
             1.  Engineering--Handbooks, manuals,
         etc. 1.Sounders, Mott, 1904- ed. II.
         Title.
  TA151.E8 1974
  ISBN 0-471-24553-4                   620'.002'02
                                           74-7467
                        H 000 018       LC-MARC3
```

FIGURE 2.2 Card Using Title

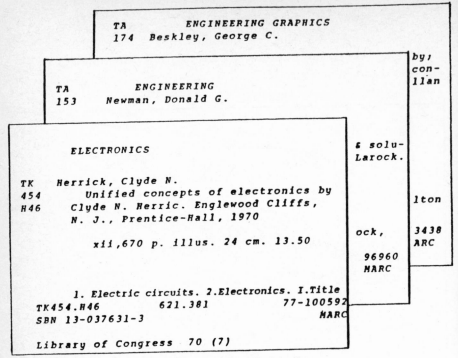

FIGURE 2.3 Cards Using Particular Subjects

Warning *If you cannot find any subject cards for your topic, it is likely that another term or phrase is used to describe the subject. Ask the reference librarian to help you use the subject authority book:* The Library of Congress Guide to Subject Headings.

• **Find Your Book in the Library.**

When you have located the catalog card, note the call number in the upper left corner. This number is what you need to find the book on the shelf. The call number begins with letters of the alphabet and is called the *Library of Congress Classification System.* (See Figure 2.4.)

The title card (Figure 2.2) and the subject card (Figure 2.3) are identical except that the subject and title are typed above the author's name.

```
Call
Number          Ref
                TA
                151    Eshbach, Ovid Wallace, 1898-1958, ed.
Author's        E8        Handbook of engineering fundamen-
Last               tals, prepared by a staff of special-
Name               ists under the editorship of Mott
                   Souders and Ovid W. Eshbach. 3d ed.
                   New York, Wiley [c1975]
                      x, 1530 p. illus. 22 cm. (Wiley
                   engineering handbook series)
                      Includes index.
                      1.Engineering--Handbooks, manuals,
                   etc.  I.Sounders, Mott, 1904- ed. II.
                   Title.
                TA151.E8 1974                  620'.002'02
                ISBN 0-471-24553-4                 74-7467
                                    000 018       LC-MARC
                                                         3
```

FIGURE 2.4 Sample Author Card in Card Catalog

2.0.3 Keep Track of Your Sources.

Keep track of your sources so that you will have an efficient filing system for your bibliography and footnotes.

    With a pen, record names of books, magazines, encyclopedias, on-line databases, microfiche, and computer call-up systems on 3-X-5-inch cards, using a separate card for each item. You can shift the cards around and alphabetize them easily.

• **Follow This Format for a Book.**

Author's full name (last name first)
Joint authors' names (if any)
Title (underlined)
Edition (if other than the first)
City of Publication
Publishing Company
Date of Publication
Call Number
Name of Library Owning Book

FIGURE 2.5 Book Source Card

Burne, R. M. and W. W. Bradly
Protective Coating of Metals
3rd. Ed.
New York, Amsterdam, and London
Reinhold Publishing Co.
1967
TA 462 B85   1967
CSM Library

FIGURE 2.6 Book Source Card Sample

- ## Follow This Format for a Magazine.

Author's full name, if given (last name first)
Joint authors' names (if any)
Title of article (in quotation marks)
Title of the magazine (underlined)
Volume number
Date of publication (in parentheses)
Inclusive page numbers

FIGURE 2.7 Magazine Article Source Card

Doyaen, Patrick S.
"Welding-Repairing the Tool Steel"
Welding Design and Fabrication
Vol. 51, No. 5
(May 1978)
82-85

FIGURE 2.8 Magazine Article Source Card Sample

- **Follow This Format for an Encyclopedia Article.**

Author's full name, if given (last name first)
Joint authors' names (if any)
Title of the article (in quotation marks)
Title of the encyclopedia (underlined)
Date of publication
Volume number (in parentheses)
Inclusive page numbers

FIGURE 2.9   Encyclopedia Article Source Card

Loebelson, Richard M.
"Growth Outlook"
<u>Collier's Encyclopedia</u>
1973
(1)
178-180

FIGURE 2.10   Encyclopedia Article Source Card Sample

2.0.4 Take Accurate Notes.

Using a pen and 4-X-6-inch cards (to distinguish from 3-X-5-inch source cards), take accurate notes. Fill out a separate card for each note and include source, page numbers, facts, figures, and information. (See Figures 2.11 and 2.12.)

It is safest to copy the information word for word to avoid *plagiarism.* (See Glossary.) Paraphrasing or summarizing can often be dangerous. An alternative to recording information on 4-X-6-inch cards is to photostat the material on the library's copying machine. Be certain to include author, source, and page number.

Identify the source at the top of the card.
List page numbers in source for each note.
Record facts, figures, and viewpoints accurately.
Copy information word for word.

FIGURE 2.11 Note Card

FIGURE 2.12 Note Card Sample

2.0.5 List Reference Materials on a Bibliography Sheet.

Any time you use other people's materials in your research, you must give credit to your sources. Using the following directions, list reference materials on a bibliography sheet at the back of your report. (See Figure 2.13.)

1. Start the bibliography on a new page as the last sheet of your report.
2. Head the page BIBLIOGRAPHY in caps, centered ($1\frac{1}{2}$ inches down).
3. Triple-space below the heading.
4. Do not indent the first line of the entry; indent succeeding lines five spaces.
5. Double-space between entries; single-space within entries.
6. List only those sources actually used in the paper and referred to in footnotes.
7. List authors with surnames (last names) first; if a book has more than one author, the names of the authors after the first one are put in normal order.
8. List entries alphabetically; if there is more than one entry by the same author (another article or book), use a long dash (about one inch) in place of the author's name in entries after the first.
9. List entries without an author alphabetically by the first word of an article or book (not including *a*, *an*, and *the*).
10. Separate important divisions with periods.
11. List inclusive pages of articles (not books).

BIBLIOGRAPHY

Brown, John. "Thermal Energy and Its Impact." Civil
    Engineering 24 (1976), 354–61.

Conover, Ewing. Energy and the Sun. New York: Harper &
    Row, 1975.

———. Harnessing the Sun. New York: Harper & Row, 1976.

Robbins, Paul H. "Engineering." The Encyclopedia Of Careers
    and Vocational Guidance. Vol. 1. Planning Your
    Career. Chicago: J. G. Ferguson Publishing Company
    (1976), 95–102, 276.

Smith, James. "The Sun Revolution." Science Today. Ed.
    Frank Goodwin, Stockton, et al. 21 (1957), 245–50.

"Timing is Everything." The Encyclopedia of Electronics.
    New York: Reinhold 14 (1962), 255–63.

Westheimer, John, Robert Alexander, James Moore. The
    Technical Revolution. Cincinnati: Riverton Press, 1980.

FIGURE 2.13   Sample Bibliography

2.0.6   Footnote Reference Materials from Bibliography.

Whenever you use somebody else's ideas, quoted directly or paraphrased in your own words, footnote your reference. (See *Plagiarism* in Glossary.)

In industry, most material is footnoted in the following simple way. (See Figure 2.14.)

1. Place the footnote on the same line at the end of the material needing footnoting.
2. Skip a space on the space bar.
3. Open the parenthesis.
4. List the author's last name (if no author, list abbreviated title).
5. Type a colon.
6. List the page number(s).
7. Close the parenthesis.

"The trend in engineering education is toward a strong preparation in the fundamentals of math and science for all engineering students, with specialized subjects coming later in the program or at the graduate level." (Robbins:276)

FIGURE 2.14   Sample Footnote

2.0.7   Develop a Reference Strategy

Develop a reference strategy so that you know how to find current information in your field. This strategy will save you time and money.

- **Start with a Dictionary.**

Use the dictionary to identify your subject and its scope. Learn to rely on technical dictionaries such as the following (The numbers on the left refer to the Library of Congress Call Numbers.):

Ref   *McGraw-Hill Dictionary of Scientific and Technical Terms.* New
Q   York, 1974.
123
M15

Ref   *Aviation & Space Dictionary.* 6th ed. Los Angeles: Aero, 1980.
TL
509
A8
1980

Ref   Markus, John. *Electronics Dictionary*. 4th ed. New York:
R   McGraw-Hill, 1978.
621.3
M
1978

• Follow Up with an Encyclopedia.

Use the encyclopedia to survey your topic: history, background, development, and current thrust. Become familiar with the specialty encyclopedias in your field.

Ref   *Van Nostrand's Scientific Encyclopedia*. 5th ed. New York: Van
Q   Nostrand-Reinhold, 1976.
121
V3
1976

Ref   *The McGraw-Hill Encyclopedia of Science and Technology*. 5th ed.
Q   New York, 1982.
121
M35
1982

Ref   Sands, Leo G. *The Encyclopedia of Electronic Circuits*. New York:
TK   Prentice-Hall, 1975.
7804
S9

• Concentrate on Handbooks and Manuals.

The handbooks and manuals in your technical field are thorough and detailed reference books that sum up the established or proven knowledge in a given field.

Ref   *Reference Data for Radio Engineers*. 6th ed. Indianapolis: Sams,
TK   1975.
6552
F4
1975

Ref   Harper, Charles A. *Handbook of Electronic Packaging*. New York:
TK   McGraw-Hill, 1969.
7870
H284

Ref   Simonson, Leroy. *Private Pilot Study Guide*. Glendale, Cal.:
TL   Aviation Book Club, 1978.
710
S54

Ref   Eshbach, Ovid W., and Mott Sanders, *Handbook of Engineering*
TA   *Fundamentals*. 3rd ed. New York: Wiley, 1975.
151
E8
1975

Ref   *Machinery's Handbook* (a reference book for the mechanical
TJ   engineer, draftsman, toolmaker, and machinist). 21st ed. New
151   York: Industrial Press, 1979.
M3
1979

• Review the Yearbooks and Almanacs.

Yearbooks and almanacs will give you new ideas, information, and facts
too new to be found in any other reference sources.

Ref   *McGraw-Hill Yearbook of Science and Technology*. New York.
Q   (Annual.)
1
M13

Ref   *Science Year*. New York: World Book. (Annual.)
Q
9
S33

Ref   *Jane's All the World's Aircraft*. New York: McGraw-Hill. (Annual.)
TL
501
J3

Ref   *Design News Annual*. Chicago: Chaners Publishing.
T
12
D4

- **Use Magazines, Newspapers, and Special Indexes.**

Decide which magazine indexes to use. Then search the indexes by subject, using the most recent and specific terms you know. If you need help in finding the material, ask the reference librarian.

> **Applied Science and Technology Index** covers all levels of scientific and technical magazines, from pure research to handyman
> **Business Periodicals Index** covers industry, big business, and finance
> **Reader's Guide to Periodical Literature** covers the most general and well-known "news stand" magazines
> **Science Citation Index** covers over 2,000 scientific and technical journals; has worldwide coverage
> **Government Reports Announcements** provides access to technical studies sponsored by the U.S. government
> **Monthly Catalog of U.S. Government Publications** provides access to all documents issued by the U.S. Congress, President, FAA, OSHA, Navy, and so on

- **Search On-Line Databases.**

Ask the reference librarian what is available in computerized information retrieval systems. If your library does not have a computerized system, check other libraries in your area.

Subject coverage is the primary consideration in on-line search. For example, you can ask NTIS (National Technical Information Service), "Is there any literature on robotic welding?" In seconds you will have a list of all the literature available.

The most popular databases are these:

> **BIOSIS Previews** (Bioscience Information Service of Biological Abstracts)
> **CA Search** (Chemical Abstracts Service)
> **ERIC** (Educational Resources Information Center)
> **MEDLINE** (National Library of Medicine)
> **NTIS** (National Technical Information Service)
> **Psychological Abstracts** (American Psychological Association)

- **Search the Microfiche.**

Ask the reference librarian if you need help in finding the material because microfiche are located in the reference section.

Where You Have Been

Information retrieval skills will make your research easier.

You have learned how to use the *access tools* in the library so that you know where to look for materials, how to find the subjects you need, how to keep track of your sources and information, how to record your information, how to write a bibliography, and how to use footnotes to give credit to your sources and to avoid plagiarism.

You have a *reference strategy*.

Exercises

1. What is the *access tool* in the library for each of the following?

   general book collection

   _____

   reference book collection

   _____

   _____

   magazines and newspapers

   _____

   audio-visual collection

   _____

   _____

   on-line databases

   _____

   _____

2. How is the card catalog cross-indexed?

   _____

   _____

   _____

   _____

3. Choose a topic in your major field. Go to the library's card catalog and locate a book. Using the instructions in this manual, record the bibliographical information.

_____

_____

_____

_____

4. Find the book in the stacks and, using the instructions in this manual, write a direct quotation from the book and correctly footnote the quotation.

_____

_____

_____

_____

5. Go to the reference section of the library and find a periodical or a journal in your major field. Using the instructions in this manual, record the bibliographical information.

_____

_____

_____

_____

_____

6. Write a direct quotation from the periodical or journal. Using the instructions in this manual, correctly footnote the quotation.

_____

_____

_____

_____

_____

7. Using instructions in this manual, list the previous two sources in correct bibliographical entries.

_____

_____

_____

_____

8. Check your school and local libraries to see if they subscribe to an on-line searching system such as NTIS (National Technical Information Source). If you locate an on-line service, look up a particular subject in your technical field, for example, semiconductors. List information from the database.

_____

_____

_____

9. Define _plagiarism._

_____

_____

10. An educated person is one who knows where to look for information when he or she needs it. Now that you have a reference strategy, pick a subject that you may want to research for a formal report and find everything you can on the subject. List the sources on 3″-X-5″ cards.

PART THREE
Learning to Write

Where You Are Going

In Part Three you are going to learn how to

- write clearly
- write concisely
- write forcefully

for a specific audience

So that you can

- describe mechanisms
- describe processes
- give instructions
- write memorandums
- write informal reports
- write formal reports
- write letters
- use graphs

3.0.1   Ask Yourself Four Important Questions.

You now have a research strategy. Your next step is to develop a writing strategy. Writing, like mathematics, is a discipline that can be learned. In Part Three you are going to learn to write clear, concise, and forceful prose.

Have a *plan* before you begin. Ask yourself four important questions: *What* am I expected to write? *Why* am I writing? *Who* is my audience? *When* is the communication due?

•   What Am I Expected to Write?

1. Description of a mechanism
2. Description of a process
3. Instructions
4. Memorandum   choose the proper format
5. Informal report
6. Formal report

•   Why Am I Expected to Write?

1. To report a study
2. To report progress on a job
3. To give instructions   know the purpose
4. To provide information
5. To make recommendations

•   Who Is My Audience?

1. A technical person
   (an initiated reader)
2. A lay person
   (an uninitiated reader)   know your audience
3. One person
4. A group of persons
   (initiated and uninitiated)

•   When Is the Communication Due?

1. Information retrieval
2. Planning   make a time schedule
3. Writing
4. Revising

3.0.2 Be Clear.

Take your reader by the eyes (if not the hand) and lead him or her through your writing by defining your terms carefully; using the transitions or bridge words; using lists, tables, and figures; and using headings and subheadings.

- ### Define Your Terms.

Use a sentence definition for a technical (initiated) audience: Name the term to be defined, give the class to which the term belongs, give the distinguishing characteristics of the term that make it different from the rest of the class, and give examples to demonstrate the meaning of the term.

An A.D. note is an Airworthiness Directive issued by the Federal Aviation Administration requiring a mandatory change for safety reasons, for example, a change in wing design because of too much stress.

FIGURE 3.1 Sentence Definition for Technical Audience

Use an extended definition for a lay (uninitiated) audience. Name the term to be defined, give the class to which the term belongs, give the distinguishing characteristics of the term that make it different from the rest of the class, compare the term with something that is familiar to the audience (an *analogy*), and give examples to demonstrate the meaning of the term.

An A.D. note is an Airworthiness Directive issued by the Federal Aviation Administration requiring a mandatory change for safety reasons. This note is similar to having your car recalled by the manufacturer because the automatic shift releases itself from a "park" position.

FIGURE 3.2 Extended Definition for Lay Audience

- ### Use Guide Posts.

Use transition (bridge words) to guide your audience with signs that go in the same direction or in another direction.

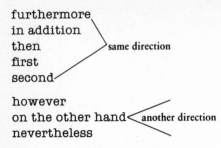

Use lists to open up the page and to make information easier for the eye to follow.

1. furthermore
2. in addition
3. then   same direction
4. first
5. second

1. however
2. on the other hand   different direction
3. nevertheless

Use headings and subheadings to differentiate between major and minor points, as in outline form.

1.0 Transitions   I.
   1.01 Same direction   A.
      1.0.1.1 furthermore   1.
      1.0.1.2 in addition   2.
      1.0.1.3 then   3.
      1.0.1.4 first   4.
      1.0.1.5 second   5.
   1.02 Different direction   B.
      1.0.2.1 however   1.
      1.0.2.2 on the other hand   2.
      1.0.2.3 nevertheless   3.

Use tables and figures to clarify and to add interest to your writing.

TABLE 3.1   Transitions

Transition	Direction
furthermore ⟶	same direction
on the other hand ⟵	different direction
however ⟵	different direction
then ⟶	same direction

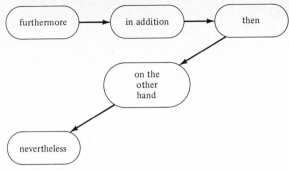

FIGURE 3.3 Transitions

3.0.3 Be Concise.

• Tell Where You Are Going.

State your findings, state your conclusions based on your findings, and state your recommendations (if any).

> This is to inform you of the status of the sheetmetal training segment of Welding Technology 221.
>
> Since we started this training program, two of our five objectives have been reached: bend allowance and layout procedures.
>
> The three areas not yet covered are pan brake operation, press brake operation, and mechanical fastening. (See Table 2.2.)

TABLE 3.2 Sheetmetal Training

Subject	Description
Bend Allowance	Material for Bend
Layout	Flat Pattern
Pan Brake	Machine Setup
Press Brake	Machine Setup
Mechanical Fasteners	Types of Fasteners

> To complete the three remaining areas, I suggest that lab time be used for the following reasons: All bid jobs will be completed by 21 April 1980, and final MIG testing will be completed by 22 April 1980.

• Go There.

Give an exact point-by-point account of the work that led to the findings, the conclusions, and the recommendations.

The subject area breakdown is based on a careful analysis of the difficulty level of materials to be covered in the allotted time span available.

The optimum subject area breakdown to complete the sheet-metal training is, therefore, the one shown in Table 3.3.

TABLE 3.3   Subject Area Breakdown

Subject	Dates
Pan Break	22 April– 7 May
Press Brake	8 May –21 May
Mechanical Fasteners	22 May – 5 June
Final Testing	7 June

- **Tell Where You Have Been.**

Restate findings, conclusions, and recommendations. This is the most emphatic spot in your report. Make it persuasive.

> As I have stated, two of our five objectives have been reached: head allowance and layout procedures. The three areas not yet covered are pan brake operation, press brake operation, and mechanical fastening.
>
> Successful completion of this last segment on dates shown will provide the student with sufficient knowledge to perform light manufacturing duties.

3.0.4   Be Forceful.

Take pride in your work. Remember that your personality, which is your effect on other people, shows every time you write; so do a perfect job.

Think of a 35mm slide show: Give your audience a little bit of copy, give it some white space, give a little bit of copy, and give some white space. Your writing will be attractive, pleasing to the eye, and forceful.

- Use a good quality $8\frac{1}{2}$-X-11-inch paper (20-pound rag).
- Type on one side only.
- Use double spacing throughout.
- Leave adequate white space and margins of from 1 inch to $1\frac{1}{2}$ inches at top, bottom, and sides, particularly on the left-hand side.
- Type the title two or three inches from the top of the page on which the text begins.
- Proofread carefully to eliminate all noise.

- Revise if necessary.
- Turn in a perfect paper.

MURPHY'S LAW

1. Nothing is ever as easy as it looks.
2. Everything will take longer than you think it will.
3. If anything can possibly go wrong, it will.

ASWELL'S ADJUNCT

Even if nothing can possibly go wrong, something will.

FIGURE 3.4

HOW TO DESCRIBE A MECHANISM

1.0 INTRODUCTION (Tell Where You Are Going)

In one paragraph tell what the mechanism does, what it looks like, what parts it has, and who will use it and why.

In alphabetical order, list and define any special terms or words, depending on who the audience is.

2.0 PARTS IN DETAIL (Go There)

In one sentence briefly state the main parts of the mechanism.

2.1 List the main parts of the mechanism (top to bottom, left to right, clockwise).
2.2 Describe each part in detail (shape, size, material, location, finish, color, and any other characteristics). Use tables and figures wherever possible and place them near the copy.

3.0 SUMMARY (Tell Where You Have Been)

Summarize what the mechanism does, what it looks like, what parts it has, and who will use it and why. (Restate the introduction in more emphatic terms.)

Model of Mechanism Description

THE INTEL 2716 EPROM

1.0 INTRODUCTION

The Intel 2716 is a 16,384 bit E̲raseable, P̲rogram-
mable R̲ead-O̲nly M̲emory consisting of the case, the
integrated circuit, 24 connecting pins, and a quartz window. The 2716 is used by engineers, research and development (R&D) technicians, and hobbyists for prototype
development, because the EPROM can be programmed
and erased over and over again.

2.0 PARTS IN DETAIL

The 2716 is composed of a case, 24 connecting pins,
the integrated circuit (IC), and a quartz window. (See
Figure 1.)

2.1 List of Parts

    1. Case

    2. Connecting pins

    3. Integrated circuit

    4. Quartz window

1

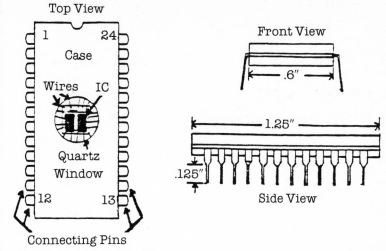

Figure 1   Part Locations

(Intel:8-5)

2.2   Detailed Parts Description

2.2.1   Case

The case is the largest component in the 2716 because it houses all the other parts. It measures 1.25 inches by .6 inch. It is usually made of hermetically sealed plastic or two ceramic halves epoxied together. The color is black, gray, or white.

2

2.2.2   Connecting Pins

The connecting pins are made of tin-plated copper. There are two rows of 12 pins each. Each pin is .1 inch from the next, and the rows are .6 inch apart. Tiny wires are welded between the 24 connecting pins and the IC.

2.2.3   Integrated Circuit

The integrated circuit is located at the center of the case. It is made of a block of silicon .25 inch square and about .05 inch high. The IC has a metallic silver color.

2.2.4   Quartz Window

The quartz window is a clear piece of quartz .3 inch in diameter. It is located directly above the IC.

3.0   SUMMARY

The Intel 2716 16K EPROM is an electronic memory chip made with a case, 24 connecting pins, an integrated circuit, and a quartz window. The 2716 is used by engineers, R&D technicians, and hobbyists in prototype

computer development because it can be programmed

and reprogrammed over and over again.

BIBLIOGRAPHY

MCS-80 User's Manual. Intel Corp. October 1977 (6-60 to
    6-63, 8-5).

HOW TO DESCRIBE A PROCESS

1.0 INTRODUCTION (Tell Where You Are Going)

In one paragraph state the process you are describing, briefly list the major steps in chronological order, and tell who will use this process.

In alphabetical order list and define any special terms or words, depending on who the audience is. Use tables and figures whenever possible and place them near the copy.

2.0 STEPS IN DETAIL (Go There)

In one sentence state the main steps of the process.

2.1 List the main steps.
2.2 Describe each step in detail. (What? Where? When? Why?)

3.0 SUMMARY (Tell Where You Have Been)

Summarize the entire process, list the major steps, and tell who will use the process and why. (Restate the introduction in more emphatic terms.)

Model of Process Description

DETERMINING THE OHMIC VALUE OF RESISTORS

1.0 INTRODUCTION

Determining the ohmic value of resistors is a quick and easy process determined by finding the values of four color bands painted around the resistor body near one end. Each color represents a number from zero to nine. (See Table 1.) The values of the first and second bands are multiplied by the value of the third band, and tolerance is determined. Electronics technicians can easily calculate the ohmic value of resistors in order to drop the voltage from a power supply to the necessary value.

You will need to know the following definitions:

The ohm is the unit measurement for resistance. (Angerbauer:18)

Resistance is the opposition which a material or a device offers to electric current. (Angerbauer:17)

The tolerance of a resistor is the percentage of error (±) in the ohmic value of that resistor.

1

TABLE 1   Carbon Resistor Color Code

	1st Band	2nd Band	No. Zeros	Multiply by	Tolerance (%)
Black	0	0	0	1	
Brown	1	1	1	10	
Red	2	2	2	100	
Orange	3	3	3	1,000	
Yellow	4	4	4	10,000	
Green	5	5	5	100,000	
Blue	6	6	6	1,000,000	
Violet	7	7	7	10,000,000	
Gray	8	8	8	100,000,000	
White	9	9	9	1,000,000,000	
Gold	—	—	—	0.1	5 percent
Silver	—	—	—	0.01	10 percent

(Angerbauer:32)

2.0   STEPS IN DETAIL

The values of the first two colored bands are multiplied by the value of the third colored band, and the tolerance is determined.

2.1   List of Steps

1. Determining the value of the first band

2. Determining the value of the second band

3. Multiplying by the value of the third band

4. Determining tolerance

2

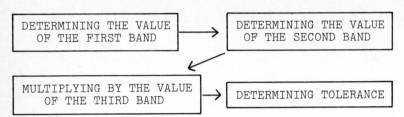

Figure 1   Determining the Ohmic Value of Resistors

2.2   Detailed Description

2.2.1   Determining the Value of the First Band

The value of the first band is determined by identifying the color of the band painted closest to one end of the resistor. (See Figure 2.) By referring to a color-code chart, as in Table 1, one can identify the numerical value of that color. That number represents the first significant digit. For example, 1 is the first significant digit of 15.

2.2.2   Determining the Value of the Second Band

The second band is the band that immediately follows the first. The numerical value of the second colored band is determined by referring to a color-code chart, as in Table 1. That number represents the second significant digit. For example, 5 is the second significant digit of 15.

2.2.3   Multiplying by the Value of the Third Band

By referring to a color-code chart, as in Table 1, one identifies the numerical value of the third colored band, which immediately follows the second. The first two significant digits are multiplied by the value of the third colored band. This third calculation gives the ohmic value of the resistor.

2.2.4   Determining Tolerance

After the ohmic value of the resistor is determined, the tolerance is determined by multiplying the ohmic value of the resistor by the value of the fourth colored band. (See Table 1.) For example, if the ohmic

value of the resistor were 15 ohms and the tolerance

were 5 percent (gold), the resistor would have a

tolerance of 0.75 ohms: $15 \times .05 = .75$.

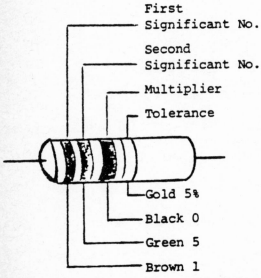

First
Significant No.

Second
Significant No.

Multiplier

Tolerance

Gold 5%

Black 0

Green 5

Brown 1

Figure 2   15-Ohm Resistor with 5 Percent Tolerance

3.0 SUMMARY

Resistors are the most common elements used in

electronic circuits. They come in many different ohmic

values. The Electronics Industries Association

established a color code (see Table 1) to enable techni-

cians, with practice, to determine quickly and easily the

ohmic value of resistors. Four color-coded bands are

painted around the resistor body, and each color repre-

sents a number from zero to nine. The values of the

first two colored bands are multiplied by the value of

the third colored band, and the tolerance is calculated by

finding the value of the fourth band, multiplied by the

ohmic value of the resistor.

BIBLIOGRAPHY

Angerbauer, George J. Principles of DC and AC Circuits. Boston: Breton Publishers, 1978.

HOW TO GIVE INSTRUCTIONS

1.0 INTRODUCTION (Tell Where You Are Going)

In one paragraph tell what it is you are explaining, tell who will use these instructions, and describe any needed equipment or skills.

In one sentence briefly list the main steps.

In alphabetical order list and define any special words, depending on your audience.

2.0 STEPS IN DETAIL (Go There)

In one sentence state the main steps.

2.1 List the main steps.
2.2 Describe each step in detail. Use tables and figures whenever possible and place them near the copy.

3.0 SUMMARY (Tell Where You Have Been)

Summarize the instructions, list the major steps, and tell who will use these instructions. Describe the equipment or skills necessary. (Restate the introduction in more emphatic terms.)

Model of Instructions

INSTRUCTIONS FOR FINDING TRUE HEADING AND
GROUND SPEED BY USING A FLIGHT COMPUTER

1.0 INTRODUCTION

To find the true heading and ground speed, the
pilot uses the wind side of a flight computer. A pencil
and a flight computer are needed. These are the main
steps: Set the wind direction, plot the wind speed, set
the true course, determine the wind correction angle,
read the true heading, and determine the ground speed.

Definitions

1. Flight computer—a portable type of slide rule used
by pilots to compute true headings,
ground speed, distance traveled in
a period of time, fuel consumption,
and so on

2. Ground speed   —the speed of the airplane relative
to the ground (1:A:13)

3. True airspeed   —the actual speed of the plane
through the air

1

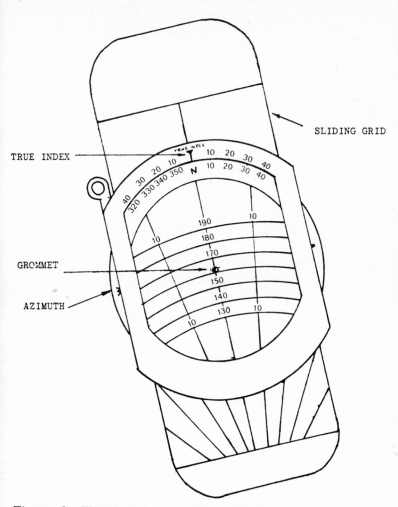

SLIDING GRID

TRUE INDEX

GROMMET

AZIMUTH

Figure 1   Flight Computer (Simplified Diagram)
(Aviation Fundamentals, 1972)

2

4. <u>True heading</u>   —the direction that an aircraft is actually heading, as measured in degrees from true north (1:8:9)

5. <u>Wind correction</u> — the angle correction needed to compen-
<u>angle</u>   sate for drift caused by the wind

2.0   STEPS IN DETAIL

Set the wind direction, plot the wind speed, set the true course, determine the wind correction and angle, read the true heading, and determine the ground speed.

2.1   <u>List of Steps</u>

1. Set wind direction.

2. Plot wind speed.

3. Set true course.

4. Determine wind correction angle.

5. Read true heading.

6. Determine ground speed.

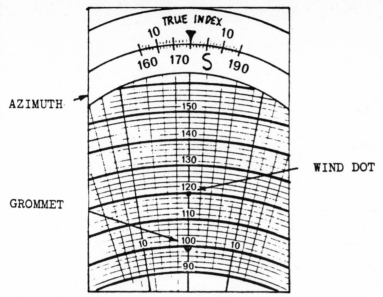

Figure 2   Plotting the Wind Speed

2.2   Steps in Detail

2.2.1   Set the Wind Direction

Given information:

True course   —90°

True airspeed —100 mph

Wind direction—175°

Wind velocity —20 mph

Set the wind direction of 175° by rotating the aximuth

until 175° reads directly under the true index. (See

Figure 2.)

4

2.2.2 Plot the Wind Speed (Velocity)

Slide the grid through the computer until the grommet is on one of the heavy lines extending from left to right. Place the wind velocity on the azimuth face by placing a pencil mark 20 miles (mph) from the grommet. This mark is called a wind dot. Each horizontal arc represents 2 mph. Each vertical line represents 2°. (See Figure 2.)

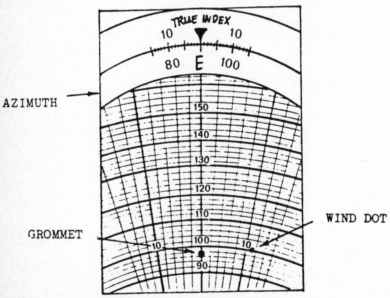

Figure 3   Setting the True Course

5

2.2.3 Set the True Course

Place the true course of 90° under the true index. With the true course under true index, slide the grid until the pencil mark, or wind dot, is positioned on the true airspeed line of 100 mph. (See Figure 3.)

2.2.4 Determine the Wind Correction Angle

Find the wind correction angle by checking the number of vertical lines (degrees) to the left or right (in this case to the right) between the grid center line and the wind dot. The wind correction angle is 11° to the right. (See Figure 3.)

2.2.5 Read the True Heading

To find the true heading, the scales on either side of the true index are used. Since the correction angle is 11° to the right, start at the true index symbol and count 11 units to the right. Read the true heading directly under the eleventh unit. The true heading is 111°. If the wind dot is to the left, count left for the true heading.

6

2.2.6   Determine the Ground Speed

Without moving the computer setting, read the ground speed under the grommet. In this case, the ground speed is 97 mph. For more problems, see Figure 4.

3.0 SUMMARY

A flight computer is a must for all pilots, especially for determining true heading and ground speed. The steps are as follows: Set the wind direction, plot the wind speed, set the true course, determine the wind correction angle, read the true heading, and determine the ground speed.

SAMPLE PROBLEMS

WIND		TRUE COURSE	TRUE AIR- SPEED	WIND CORRECTION ANGLE	TRUE HEADING	GROUND SPEED
DIRECTION	VELOCITY					
degrees	mph	degrees	mph	degrees	degrees	mph
135	30	240	120	14 L	226	124
215	20	260	130	6 L	254	115
050	33	260	150	6 R	266	178
330	45	350	150	6 R	344	107
300	45	100	150	6 L	94	191
220	30	130	150	12 R	142	147

Figure 4   (Pilot's Handbook of Aeronautical Knowledge, 1971)

The wind direction, wind velocity, true course, and true
airspeed are usually given. The pilot determines the
wind correction angle, true heading, and ground speed
by using the given information. A flight computer is
needed for these problems.

8

BIBLIOGRAPHY

Federal Aviation Administration. Pilot's Handbook of
    Aeronautical Knowledge. Washington, D.C.: U.S.
    Government Printing Office, 1971.

Sanderson, Jeppeson. Aviation Fundamentals. Denver,
    Col.: Jeppeson Sanderson, Inc., 1972.

A written informal message within a company—
office to office,
office to field—
to request information,
confirm an order or a conversation,
report a conclusion,
and/or
make a
recommendation

FIGURE 3.5 A Memorandum

HOW TO WRITE A MEMORANDUM

1.0 TELL WHERE YOU ARE GOING

State the findings.
State the conclusions (if any).
State the recommendations (if any) based on the findings.

2.0 GO THERE

Give an exact point-by-point account in chronological order of the work

2.1 that led to the findings,
2.2 that led to the conclusions,
2.3 that led to the recommendations. Use tables and figures wherever
 needed and place them near the copy.

3.0 TELL WHERE YOU HAVE BEEN

Summarize the subject matter of the memorandum.
Restate the findings.
Restate the conclusions (if any).
Restate the recommendations (if any).

Model of Memorandum

MEMORANDUM

TO: Louis Defreitas, Supervisor   DATE: 2 May 198_
FROM: Mario D. Silva, Technician
PURPOSE: Recommended Procedures for Making an Open
           Root Butt Weld (Vertical Up)

This paper is in answer of your recent request for

information regarding the welding of an open root butt

weld. The following recommendations should be followed in

order to assure satisfactory results. Since I was not given

any job specifications, I will deal with butt welds in general.

Before one begins the welding process, the machine

current should be set for the thickness of metal being

welded. This can be achieved by running a bead in the flat

position on a piece of scrap which is the same thickness as

the original pieces. After the correct current is set for the

flat position, the current is cut back 30 to 55 amperes for

welding vertical up.

It is extremely important to prepare the plates prop-

erly. The preparation of the joint for metals up to $\frac{1}{8}$ inch

1

in thickness requires matching the sheets by a distance to the metal's thickness. Regardless of metal thickness, in any type of butt joint the penetration through the base metal must be 100 percent.

In order to achieve full melt-thru on the root pass, the weldor uses a whipping motion. It is important that the slag from previous weld passes is cleaned. (See Figure 1.)

The welding speed for this joint will be determined by the diameter of the electrode being used. In order to cut down on labor I suggest using the largest electrode diameter feasible. The larger electrode will fill the joint rapidly. This in turn will decrease the cost of making this joint.

For your benefit I have constructed a graph on welding speeds for various electrode diameters. It should be noted that these values are based on maximum speeds possible with each individual electrode diameter. (See Figure 2.)

In conclusion, I recommend some safety precautions that <u>if followed</u> will prevent personal injury and equipment damage:

2

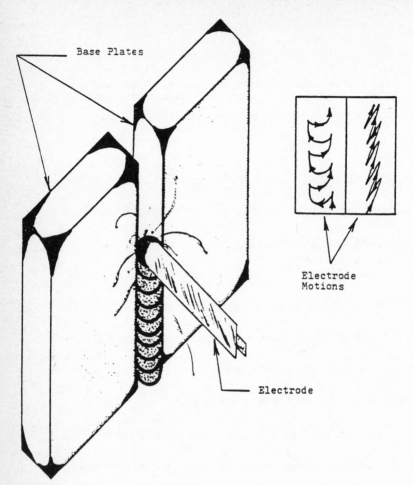

Figure 1   Joint Configuration

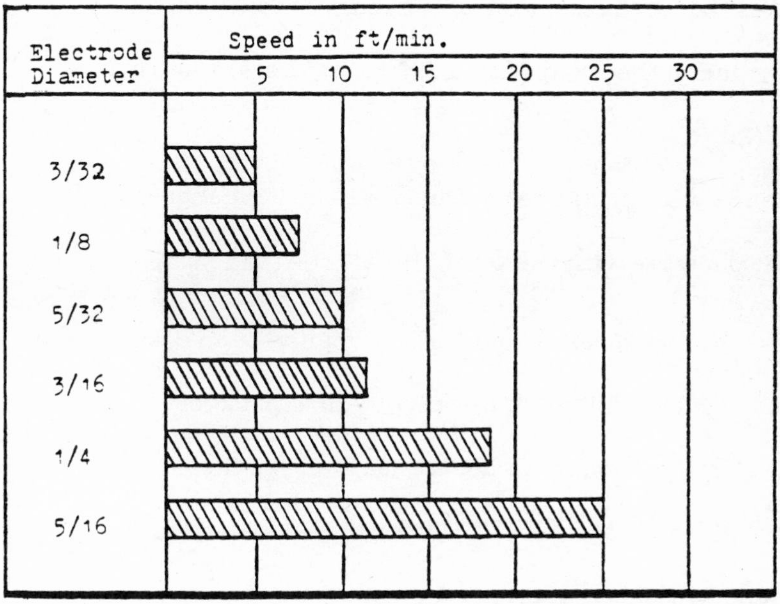

Electrode Diameter	Speed in ft/min.					
	5	10	15	20	25	30
3/32						
1/8						
5/32						
3/16						
1/4						
5/16						

Figure 2   Welding Speeds for Electrodes   (Modern Welding, 1976:43)

4

1. All the welders who will be performing the welding should have correct protective clothing.

2. Welders should not be permitted to use oily, greasy, ragged clothing.

3. Safety glasses should be worn under the welding helmet. This is a safety precaution which <u>must be</u> followed, according to the Occupational Safety and Hazard Association (OSHA).

4. Once the welding has been completed, the joint should be marked clearly with the word "HOT."

If these recommendations for the welding of an open root butt weld are followed, we will obtain satisfactory results. Furthermore, if our department follows the recommended safety precautions, we can eliminate personal injury and equipment damage.

HOW TO WRITE AN
INFORMAL REPORT

(Progress report, periodic report, travel report, study report, or any other report of an informal nature)

1.0 INTRODUCTION (Tell Where You Are Going)

State the purpose of the report.
State your findings to date that justify conclusions and recommendations (note importance of *tone*), if any. (See the Glossary.)
State your conclusions and/or recommendations based on your findings.

2.0 DISCUSSION (Go There)

In one sentence state the scope (plan) of the report.
Give an exact point-by-point account in the chronological order of the work

2.1 that led to the findings (noted and footnoted),
2.2 that led to the conclusions (noted and footnoted),
2.3 that led to the recommendations. Use tables and figures wherever needed and place them near the copy.

3.0 CONCLUSION (Tell Where You Have Been)

Summarize the subject matter of the report.
Restate the findings.
Restate the conclusions.
Restate the recommendations (if any).

Model of Informal Report

⊡ E-Systems

TO: J. Bell   DATE: 20 November 198_
          Quality Control Manager
FROM: G. Meers
          Quality Control Technician
SUBJECT: Recall of Computer Chips

1.0   INTRODUCTION

E-Systems is the fastest growing producer of elec-

tronic systems in Silicon Valley. This rapid growth can

be attributed to our production of quality products

through regular observance of quality control procedures.

During the past week, four batches of computer

chips have been recalled. After thorough research, I

have located the source of the problem: The X gain

setting on our oscilloscopes was slipping out of calibra-

tion when the time/cm setting was changed, causing

them to give inaccurate readings.

Therefore I recommend that all technicians be

officially instructed to recalibrate the oscilloscope's X

gain setting after changing the time/cm setting.

2.0   DISCUSSION

The number of computer chips recalled is in excess of that allowed by our quality control guidelines; therefore I researched the problem thoroughly. My research included determining which work shifts made the erroneous readings, meeting with the department manager, checking the calibration procedures, meeting with the maintenance foreman, and verifying the findings.

2.1   Order of Research

1. Determining which work shifts made the erroneous readings

2. Meeting with the department manager

3. Checking the calibration procedures

4. Meeting with the maintenance foreman

5. Verifying findings

2.2   Research Details

2.2.1   Determining Which Work Shifts Made the Erroneous Readings

By identifying the label coding on the four batches of recalled computer chips, it was determined that all

2

three shifts had processed computer chips with erroneous oscilloscope readings. (See Table 1.)

TABLE 1   Package Coding

Product	Date	Shift Code	Shift
ES 100	03-11-81	01	Day
ES 100	03-11-81	02	Evening
ES 100	04-11-81	03	Swing
ES 100	04-11-81	01	Day

(Trupp:203)

2.2.2   Meeting With the Department Manager

I met with Mr. Jones, the department manager, to
determine if the oscilloscopes are being calibrated. Mr.
Jones assured me that all oscilloscopes are being calibrated at the beginning of each shift.

2.2.3   Checking the Calibration Procedures

I constructed a list of the calibration procedures
and then met with each shift foreman to determine if
the oscilloscopes are being calibrated properly. All three
shift foremen assured me that their technicians are
familiar with the calibration procedures and all steps
are being followed. (See Table 2.)

3

TABLE 2   Steps for Calibration of Oscilloscopes

Control	Visual	Setting
1. Brillance	↺	Full CCW, Power Off
2. Focus	↑	Center of Rotation
3. Astig	↑	Center of Rotation
4. Trig Level	↺	Full CCW Auto
5. Stability	↻	Full CW
6. Trig Selector	⋮	Normal, +, INT
7. X Shift	↑	Center of Rotation
8. X Gain	↺	Full CCW
9. Time/cm	↺×5ms	5 MS
10. Variable	↻	Full CW
11. Y Shift	↑	Center of Rotation
12. Vernier	↑	Center of Roation
13. Volts/cm	×↺ 10mv	10 mv
14. Variable	↻	Full CW
15. Input	◎ Lower Left	BNC Connector

(Bertini:68)

2.2.4   Meeting With Maintenance Foreman

I contacted Mr. Smith, the maintenance foreman, and arranged to have him check the oscilloscopes for mechanical malfunctions. Mr. Smith carefully checked each oscilloscope and found that the X gain setting is slipping out of calibration when the time/cm setting is changed.

4

2.2.5 Verifying Findings

Mr. Smith and I went through the testing procedures for a computer chip on one of our oscilloscopes. When we switched the time/cm setting from 5 ms to 10 ms, the X gain setting slipped out of calibration, causing the voltage/cm reading to be incorrect.

3.0 CONCLUSION

The recall of four batches of computer chips was caused by the X gain setting on our oscilloscopes slipping out of calibration when the time/cm setting was changed, causing them to give inaccurate readings. Therefore I have instructed all technicians to recalibrate the X gain setting when the time/cm setting is changed.

BIBLIOGRAPHY

Bertini, Tullio. Learning Modules in Passive Circuits and Devices. San Mateo, Ca.: College of San Mateo, 1981.

Trupp, G. "Informal Report." Writing for Industry Instruction Manual, San Mateo, Ca.: College of San Mateo, 1981, 203.

6

HOW TO WRITE A FORMAL REPORT*

Page

USE CORRECT FORM

TITLE PAGE   i
    Title of report
    (in caps, centered)
    Submitted to
    Name, Title
    Department
    Date
    Submitted by
    Your name

LETTER OF TRANSMITTAL   ii
    Authorization for report
    Purpose of report
    Scope (plan) of report
    Acknowledgments

TABLE OF CONTENTS   iii
    In outline form
    Indicate headings listed
    Line leaders to page number

LIST OF FIGURES   iv
(within page, on another page, or in Appendix)
    Figures
    Tables
    Charts
    Diagrams
    Graphs
    Photographs

ABSTRACT (digest of the significant content of a report) . .   v
(200 words or fewer, single-spaced in one paragraph)
    Purpose of report
    Scope (plan) of report
    Conclusions (stress degree of success, if any)
    Recommendations (if any)

DEVELOP THE SUBJECT OF THE REPORT

1.0 INTRODUCTION (Tell Where You Are Going)   1
    State findings to date.

---

* *Who* will read the report? *What* do they want to know? *What* does the writer want to accomplish? *How* should the report be structured to meet these needs?

State conclusions and recommendations, if any, based on findings.

Define key terms (if needed for audience).

2.0 DISCUSSION (Go There). . . . .

In one paragraph state the scope (plan) of report.

Give exact point-by-point account in chronological order of work

2.1 that led to findings (noted and footnoted),

2.2 that led to conclusions (noted and footnoted),

2.3 that led to recommendations. Use tables and figures wherever needed and place them near the copy.

3.0 CONCLUSION (Tell Where You Have Been) . . . . . .

Summarize the subject matter of the report.

Restate findings.

Restate conclusions.

Restate recommendations

APPENDIXES

BIBLIOGRAPHY Choose a consistent form of footnoting in the body of report. (See Part Two.)

HELPFUL HINTS FOR STARTING THE FORMAL REPORT

1.0 SELECT A TOPIC

2.0 GO TO THE LIBRARY

   2.1 Check to see if there is enough *available* material on the topic.

      2.1.1 Check card catalogs.

      2.1.2 Check technical encyclopedias

      2.1.3 Check periodicals indexes.

      2.1.4 Check stacks and periodicals.

      2.1.5 Check with reference librarian.

3.0 TELEPHONE OR CALL ON NEARBY MANUFACTURERS to ask for literature or to set up an interview.

4.0 WRITE AN ABSTRACT (a brief description of 200 words or fewer) of your proposed report.

5.0 OBTAIN YOUR TECHNICAL INSTRUCTOR'S APPROVAL based on your abstract.

6.0 START WITH THE DISCUSSION SECTION OF THE REPORT

7.0 FILL IN FORWARD, INTRODUCTION, CONCLUSION, AND APPENDIXES.

HELPFUL HINTS FOR WRITING THE FORMAL REPORT

1.0 INTRODUCTION
The purpose of this report is . . . .
- Background of problem, history
- Scope of subject (what you plan to cover in report)
- Limitations of study (time, funds, assignment, and so on)
- Procedures used (interviews, survey, library research, and so on)
- Meaning of key terms (depending on audience)
- Conclusions and recommendations (if any)

2.0 DISCUSSION
In one sentence state the scope (plan) of the report. Give the exact point-by-point account in the chronological order of work.
2.1 Facts (noted and footnoted)
2.2 Cited authorities (noted and footnoted)
2.3 Tables and figures as needed
2.4 Lists, subheadings, numbering as needed

3.0 CONCLUSION (and recommendations, if any)
Conclusion that covers important findings in report (in descending order: most important first)
Recommendations (if any)

NOTE: Start with the DISCUSSION section. This is the body of your report. After you have finished the DISCUSSION section, fill in the INTRODUCTION, CONCLUSION, forward, appendixes, and bibliography. Proofread: Revise if necessary.

Make certain that data support your recommendations and/or conclusions.
- Organize your data.
- Graph your data.
- List your data.

Anything you can do to block out data graphically gives the readers a sense of organization, makes them feel better.

- Break the report up with subheads.
- Not only tell your readers where they are going but give them some directions.

FIGURE 3.6 The Technical Report

Model of Formal Report

ROBOTICS IN WELDING

Submitted to
Anita Lehman
for
English 420
Writing for Industry
College of San Mateo
San Mateo, California
28 May 198_

by
Mario D. Silva

5826 Bellflower Drive
Newark, California
28 May 198_

Mrs. Anita Lehman
Language Arts Division
College of San Mateo
San Mateo, California

Dear Mrs. Lehman:

In accordance with your instructions I have prepared the
following report, entitled "Robotics in Welding."

The purpose of this report is to examine the effectiveness of
robotics in the welding industry. It is assumed that the
reader has no technical background in this field. The report
begins with a general description of robotic units in order
to familiarize the reader. Once the reader has been exposed
to this new field, the report then covers the monetary and
health advantages of using welding robots rather than
manual processes. The report also deals with the economic
savings of companies that converted to robotic welding. In
conclusion, the author states that robotic welding systems
will increase productivity and lower operating costs.

As a welding major, I found this report to be extremely
helpful in enhancing my knowledge of the welding
industry. I thank you for giving me the opportunity to
research this report on robotics.

I would like to express my thanks to Louis DeFreitas,
chairman of Welding Technology at the College of San Mateo,
for his review of the technical information contained
within this report.

I sincerely hope that this report will prove to be satisfactory.

Respectfully yours,

Mario D. Silva

Mario D. Silva

TABLE OF CONTENTS

LIST OF FIGURES

ABSTRACT

The purpose of this report is to spell out the effectiveness of robotics in the welding industry. The report is divided into four major subject areas: Part I covers the fundamental design and programming of robotic systems; Part II introduces the reader to the main parts that make up the robotic welding system; Part III discusses the momentary and health advantages of using welding robots rather than manual processes; Part IV documents actual economic savings of companies that converted to robotic welding. The report concludes that robotic welding systems will increase productivity and lower operating costs.

ROBOTICS IN WELDING

1.0 INTRODUCTION

The purpose of this report is to examine the effi-
ciency of robotic welding units in the welding industry.
The art of manual welding can at times be a very te-
dious job. Nevertheless such jobs are essential to companies that deal with metal-joining processes. Therefore
this report will spell out the effectiveness of robotics in
the welding industry.

This report is in partial fulfillment of the requirements for English 420, Writing for Industry. Most of the
technical information in this report covers the basic
design of robotics in general.

Part I of this report introduces the reader to the
basic design and programming of robotic systems; Part II
reveals the main parts that make up the robotic welding
system; Part III describes the monetary and health
advantages of using welding robots rather than manual
processes; Part IV discusses the economic advantages of
using robotic welding systems and how individual companies

1

profited from their use. The report concludes that robotic

welding systems will increase productivity and lower

operating costs.

A Glossary of Terms will be found in Appendix A.

2.0 DISCUSSION

Part I of this report begins with a general descrip-

tion of robotic systems. Part II focuses on a more de-

tailed description, including diagrams of robotic units.

Part III reveals the monetary and health advantages

associated with robotics. Part IV documents the actual

economic savings of companies that converted to robotic

welding.

2.1 Part I: General Description of Robotic Systems

Today, in progressive welding facilities throughout

the world, automation serves to increase production,

quality, and control while reducing costs, operator

involvement, and space requirements. Often the task of

successfully advancing a new concept such as robotic

welding requires more than manufacturing expertise and

engineering skill. (Unimation:2)

Using a hand-held teach control, the welding robot is taught its job by literally leading it by the hand through its assigned task. Playback speeds are independent of teaching speeds; therefore operations taught slowly can be performed accurately at high speeds. It should be noted that teaching the robot is the most time-consuming process in the robotic welding system.

As has been noted, a welding robot is literally led by the hand through its assigned task. This procedure is accomplished through the use of keyboard entries, similar to typing a letter. In this process the welding head of the robot is positioned over the desired starting point. This location is then typed into the robot as position "X." From this point the welding head is then moved to the "Y" position. Once the welding robot is started, it will weld from "X" to "Y" consecutively. (Trevor:85)

I would like to point out that this is a very simple program. However weldments that require more than one pass will usually have several location points in order to guide the welding robot accurately.

3

2.2   Part II: Detailed Description of Parts

The three main parts that make up a welding robot

are as follows. (See Figure 1.)

1. Welding head

2. Machine frame

3. Positioner

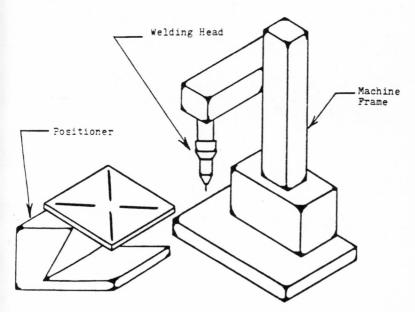

Figure 1   Robotic System   (Welding Casebook, 1979:4)

4

2.2.1   Welding Head

The welding head of most robotic units can provide a full 720° rotation with more than 60° of coordinated tilt. The torch-to-work distance can be changed quickly by a single command program. Because of these features robotic units can now be employed in down-hand and out-of-position welding. (See Figure 2.)

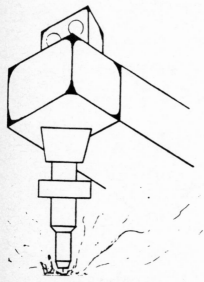

Figure 2   Welding Head   (Welding Casebook, 1979:5)

2.2.2 Machine Frame

The machine frame houses the electrical components that control the movement of the welding head. This part can also be made movable in order to aid in the positioning of the welding head. A well-built robotic unit will usually have a large frame in order to give the unit more stability.

2.2.3 Positioner

The positioner is the mechanical part of a robotic system that holds the object to be welded. This device is adjusted to coordinate part motion with torch motion. In other words, the rate at which the welding head will be feeding filler rod into the arc is equal to the rate of movement in the positioner. (Trevor:87)

The rotation and tilt axis position the weld puddle to allow down-hand position welding. This results in faster welding and better weld quality. (See Figure 3.)

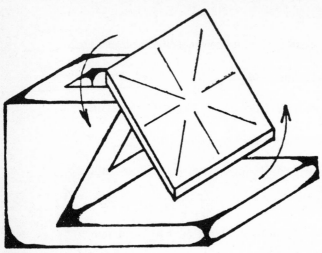

Figure 3   Positioner   <u>(Welding Casebook</u>, 1979:6)

2.3   Part III: Monetary and Health Advantages

The time a welder is actually joining metal is called

"arc time." The national average for arc time is about 30

percent. The reasons for this low rate are obvious as one

tours a shop and sees the personal protection that must be

worn and the positions required to perform the welds.

(Sullivan:3)

If a welder is paid $7.50 per hour and overhead of the

plant is 100 percent, the welder's cost is $15.00 per hour or

$31,200 per year. If his or her arc time is 30 percent, the

actual cost of the time to join metal is $31.22 divided

by 0.3, or $104,000. Obviously this is a great deal

of money. In fact, it is enough money to justify the

purchase of arc-welding robots even on a single-shift

operation. (Sullivan:4)

Today a single robotic welding unit costs $80,000 to

$100,000. Such high price ranges have limited the use of

robotic units to large manufacturing companies. These

companies can afford welding robots because through a

given period of time a welding robot will pay for itself. This

conclusion is based on production rates that have been

increased through the use of automated welding.

In other words, by producing a company's product

within a short period of time, labor costs can be lowered.

Therefore the company can in turn sell the product more

cheaply than its competition. This will result in more

contracts, more work, and larger profits. (See Figure 4.)

Welders are potentially exposed to the particulates,

gases, radiation, and noise created as byproducts of most of

the welding processes currently in use. The hazard of this

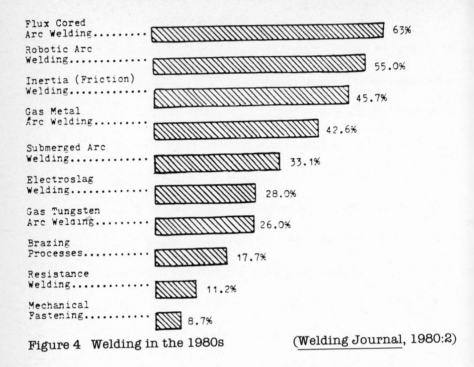

Figure 4 Welding in the 1980s   (Welding Journal, 1980:2)

exposure will depend primarily on the composition and

quantity of the fumes and gases generated and the

intensity of radiation emitted, which in turn depend on the

welding process employed and the metal being welded.

It also depends on the length of time in this type of environment and the effectiveness of control measures, such as ventilation and personal equipment. (AWS:3)

The use of robotic welding will remove the welder from such a harmful environment. A simple robotic welding setup requires the welder to be within only four feet of the actual welding. In fact once the process has been started, the welder may step back even farther than the four-foot limit. Therefore the harmful gases that are released during an arc-welding process do not come in contact with the human respiratory system. (See Figure 5.)

2.4   Part IV: Economic Savings

In order to lower costs in the manufacture of their products, the following companies investigated the possibility of automating arc welding in their shops.

In order to lower costs in the manufacture of shopping cart frames, Unarco Industries Inc. converted to robotic welding. As a result labor hours were cut to a quarter

10

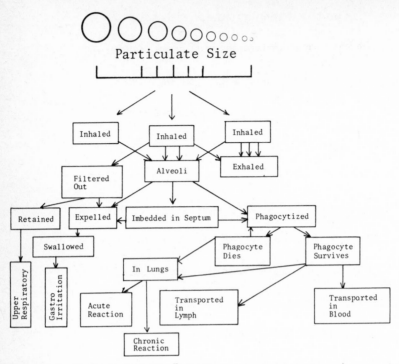

Figure 5   Particle Fate in Lungs

(Effect of Welding on Health, 1979:5)

of what they were, and a return on investment of

18 percent was among the advantages that resulted from

the conversion. In addition welds made by the robot had a

uniformly better appearance, which was an important

factor in this product. Furthermore the operator was

11

not exposed to any of the harmful welding fumes or rays. (Sullivan:6)

Still another company to profit from welding robots was AiResearch Manufacturing Company. The job taken in by this company involved the welding of traction-motor housings for self-propelled rail vehicles. Previously the welds required on this structure took five to six hours when welding was manual. However the use of a welding robot brought down the arc time to just two hours. As a result this company had a 67 percent cut in labor hours. (Sullivan:8)

These are just some of the many cases where a company discovered the monetary and health advantages of robotic welding units. In fact the automotive industry is in the process of converting to robotic welding. For example Chrysler Corporation has ordered more than 100 robots for use in welding subassemblies and assemblies on their new line of front-wheel-drive compact cars for 1980. Ford Motor Company plans to purchase 200 robots for use at two of their plants to spot weld compartment assemblies for new front-wheel-drive compact cars that will be introduced

12

in 1981. Furthermore Toyota plans to purchase some
450 additional welding robots by 1983. Obviously these
companies have become aware of the potential results that
can be expected with robotic welding.

3.0   CONCLUSION

As was previously mentioned, arc welding is a
dangerous and unhealthy job. The smoke and fumes can
cause respiratory problems and some are even toxic or
carcinogenic. As a result, more and more pressure is
being put upon management to protect people in welding.

Welding, unlike some other unpleasant jobs, requires
skilled personnel. Usually a high degree of skill is
required in out-of-position welding. For example, welding
of pressure vessels, nuclear power plants, and aircraft
parts all require the welder to pass strict tests to prove
his or her qualification.

Consequently the welding industry is worried about
the future of welding. The main body of this report
listed some of the companies that realized how robotic
welding may be the answer to the welding problems of today.

13

Welding robots offer ease of teaching, quick programming, high accuracy, and repeatability. Furthermore they work consistently and without fatigue or boredom. Most of all, they increase productivity and lower operating costs.

APPENDIX A

GLOSSARY

Carcinogenic . . . .   an agent causing or inciting cancer

Down-hand welding . . . . . .   in a descending direction of travel

Out-of-position welding . . . .   any welding that is not in the flat position

Program . . . .   coded instructions for a mechanism

Robotic . . . .   something guided by automatic controls

Weld puddle . . . .   the area of welding where the metal is still molten

BIBLIOGRAPHY

Effect of Welding on Health. New York: American Welding
    Society, 1979.

"Health Hazards of Arc Welding." Welding Journal, 1977,
    380–85.

Johnson, Nick. Interview. 12 May 1980.

"Robots for Arc Welding." Welding Journal, 1980, 28–31.

Sullivan, Mortimer. Industrial Robots. New York: Ad-
    vanced Robotics Corp., 1980.

Trevor, Davies. Robots in Industry. New York: McGraw-
    Hill, 1975.

Welding Casebook. Chicago: Unimation Inc., 1979, 2–12.

16

HOW TO WRITE LETTERS

You may be expected to write letters of inquiry, orders, sales, and/or customer relations, all requiring different formats and writing techniques for different audiences. Many businesses have their own stylebooks and will want you to follow their formats and techniques.

However, good writing is good writing regardless of the format. Use the same instructions for good writing that you have learned in this manual:

- Be clear. 　tell where you are going

- Be concise. 　go there

- Be forceful. 　tell where you have been

- Be correct. 　revise, revise, revise

your tone or attitude shows - Be polite.

Layout forms may vary, but most businesses use block, modified block, or full block form. (See the models on the next three pages.)

Model of Block Layout Form

---

mailing *address* *date*	2419 Sharon Oaks Dr. Menlo Park, CA 94025 9 April 198_

inside
address

Dr. Herbert E. Krugman
The General Electric Company
Stamford, Connecticut   06431

saluta-
tion

Dear Dr. Krugman:

Thank you for your generous help in researching industry's communication needs.

As a result of the findings, I have decided to set up a WORD MANAGEMENT consulting firm and offer my services to Bay Area industries and their employees.

I appreciate your kindness and will keep you informed of my progress.

complimentary
closing   Sincerely,

Anita J. Lehman

signature   Anita J. Lehman

Model of Modified Block Layout Form

2419 Sharon Oaks Dr.
Menlo Park, CA 94025
7 June 198_

Jeremy Cowan, Chief Engineer
Jason Rogers Engineering Company
20 Pine Street
Redwood City, California 94063

Dear Mr. Cowan:

the first
line of
each
paragraph
is
indented

    I enjoyed our meeting on 12 April and look
forward to helping your engineering staff improve
their communication skills.

    Writing, like mathematics, is a skill that
can be learned. Within a short time you will
see a marked improvement in engineering reports.

Sincerely,

Anita J. Lehman

Anita J. Lehman

Model of Full Block Layout Form

---

20 Pine Street
Redwood City, CA 94403
10 September 198_

Ms. Anita Lehman
Word Management
2419 Sharon Oaks Drive
Menlo Park, California 94025

Dear Ms. Lehman:

all lines
are flush
with
left-hand
margin

I am happy to report that the engineering staff's
writing has shown marked improvement. The reports
are clear, concise, and correct.

Thank you for your help. I shall recommend your
services to all who need them.

Sincerely,

Jeremy Cowan
Jeremy Cowan

HOW TO USE GRAPHICS

Graphics are classified as tables and figures. Each type of graphic is used for a specific purpose and presents information clearly and attractively. Many computers can translate verbal information into tables and figures with the punch of a button.

Graphics will enhance your written reports. Learn how to use tables and figures such as bar graphs, pie charts, line graphs, and flow charts.

Drawings and photographs are other visuals that can be used effectively in your reports to make your message clearer and more forceful.

• Tables (present relationships and comparisons of data)

1. Refer to the table in the body of the report after the description of it appears in words, for example, see Table 4.
2. Place the number and title above the table at the left in upper and lower case letters.
3. Add brief explanatory material in the legend below the table if necessary.
4. At bottom right give credit to the source and include the page number.
5. For clarity use adequate white space between columns.

TABLE 3.4   Sample Table

Element No.	Maximum g	Minimum g	Average g	Spread in. g
1	2.31	1.75	2.03	1.56
	2.30	1.75	2.03	1.60
2	2.58	2.45	2.46	1.33
	2.60	2.33	2.46	1.38
3	3.18	2.69	2.93	1.59
	3.22	2.68	2.92	1.64
4	3.17	2.70	2.94	1.57
	3.20	2.70	2.95	1.60

Legend: Average Spread 1.45   (Lehman:101)

• **Figures**

Bar graphs present easily constructed single-scale comparisons.

1. Decide on a scale.
2. Measure the height of each bar.
3. Draw the lines for each bar.
4. Shade in the bars.
5. Add borders.
6. Fill in appropriate headings.
7. At bottom left give figure number and title in upper and lower case letters; at bottom right give credit to source and include the page number.

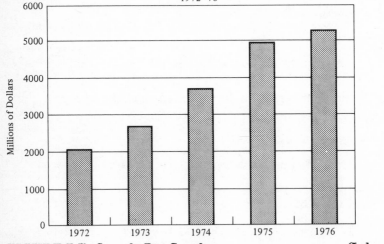

FIGURE 3.7 Sample Bar Graph   (Lehman:102)

Pie charts show percentage distribution of the whole.

1. Draw a circle by using a compass.
2. Decide on a scale to show percentages of 2 percent or more of whole.
3. Measure off the width of each segment of the circle (begin at the 12 o'clock position and move clockwise, starting with the largest quantity).
4. Draw a line for each segment with a compass and a protractor.
5. Label percentages within the circle.
6. Fill in appropriate headings.
7. At bottom left give the figure number and title; at bottom right give credit to the source and include the page number.

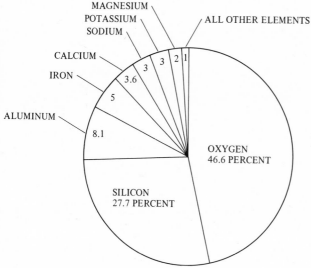

FIGURE 3.8 Sample Pie Chart   (Lehman:103)

Line graphs show a trend or movement in time periods.

1. Decide on a scale.
2. Plot time in days, months, and years on the X-axis, the horizontal line.
3. Place the magnitude or variable on the Y-axis, the vertical line.
4. Add a border.
5. Fill in appropriate headings.
6. At bottom left place the figure number and title; at bottom right give credit to the source and include the page number.

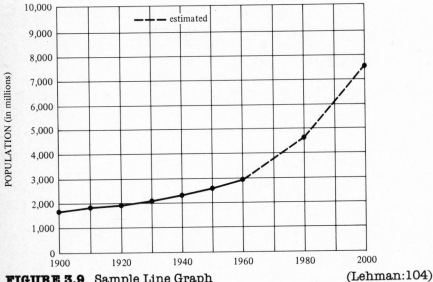

FIGURE 3.9 Sample Line Graph   (Lehman:104)

Flow charts represent steps in a process or a function to be executed.

1. Plot the correct number of boxes or circles.
2. Connect the boxes or circles with lines and arrows showing consecutive movement from one to the other.
3. Label the boxes and circles.
4. Add a border.
5. Fill in appropriate headings.
6. At bottom left place the figure number and title; at bottom right give credit to the source and include the page number

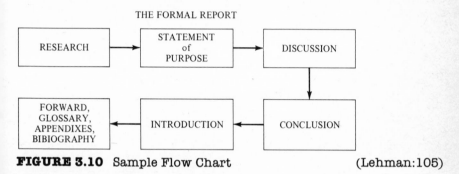

FIGURE 3.10 Sample Flow Chart (Lehman:105)

Where You Have Been

You have learned to

- describe a mechanism and a process
- give instructions
- write a memorandum, an informal report, a formal report
- use tables and figures

You have learned how to write clearly, concisely, and forcefully.

You have learned how to think logically: to tell where you are going, to go there, and to tell where you have been.

You have learned how to write for industry for upward job mobility.

Exercises

1. What four questions should you ask yourself before you start to write?

_____

_____

_____

2. For a *technical* audience define a term that you use in your major field.

_____

_____

_____

_____

3. For a lay audience, define a term that you use in your technical field.

_____

_____

_____

_____

4. In sentence form give two examples of jargon that you use in your technical field.

_____

_____

5. Translate the preceding jargon into clear, concise language.

_____

_____

6. List some transitions (bridge words) that you can use to make your report flow smoothly.

_____

_____

_____

_____

7. What do lists, tables, figures, headings, subheadings, and numbering do for a technical report?

_____

_____

_____

8. Assume that you are the lab instructor in your technical field. For a technical audience describe a tool or mechanism that you use in the laboratory. Include a figure of the tool or mechanism.

9. Assume that you are working as a technican in your technical field. For a lay audience describe a process that your firm specializes in producing. Include a flow chart of the process.

10. Write a set of user instructions for a new video game that you have invented. Figure out who the audience is, and use graphics.

11. Assume you are working as a technician on the day shift in your technical field. Write a set of instructions for the technician who will continue your work on the swing shift. Include a table listing step numbers, description of instructions, and equipment needed in each step.

12. You are an instructor in your technical field. Write a set of instructions for a process that you are teaching in the lab. Use graphics to enhance your instructions.

13. Write a memorandum to your supervisor informing him or her of the progress you are making on a project. Include a figure or table.

14. Write a memorandum to an instructor in your technical field informing him or her of the progress you are making on an assignment. Include figures and tables of your choice.

15. Assume that you are working as a technician in your technical field. You have observed over the past six months that a mechanism or a process could be improved. Using appropriate figures or tables, write an informal report to your supervisor to this effect. (Note the importance of tone.)

16. With the advice of an instructor in your technical field, research the feasibility of some mechanism, process, plan, project, or topic in which you are interested and write a formal report, using the format and instructions in this manual. Be certain that your instructor signs the agreement and approves the topic, abstract, rough draft, and completed report. (See page 108.)

17. Write a letter to an agency or company requesting helpful information for your formal report. State what you need and why you are writing.

DUE DATES

Assignment	Due Date
Topic Approval	
Abstract	
(Summary of 200 words or fewer)	
Rough Draft of Discussion Section	
Completed Rough Draft	
Finished Report	

Agreement with Instructor in Technical Department
(to be turned in with formal report)

I agree to work with _____
(your name)

on the technical content of his/her formal report.

_____
(Instructor's Signature)

_____

I approve topic   _____
(Instructor's Signature)

I approve abstract   _____
(Instructor's Signature)

I approve rough draft   _____
(Instructor's Signature)

I approve final report _____
(Instructor's Signature)

PART FOUR
Technical Writing Stylebook

Where You Are Going

In Part Four you are going to learn

- the purpose of the technical writing stylebook
- abbreviations used in industry
- capitalization
- correct usage
  - •• the exact word
  - •• the simple word
  - •• correct pronouns
  - •• numerals
  - •• parallel structure
  - •• punctuation
  - •• spelling
  - •• verb forms

4.0.1   The Purpose of the Technical Writing Stylebook

You have learned the skill of organizing your reports by using simple *deductive logic*. Now you must learn to write correctly so that your reports are not filled with disruptive noise: spelling errors, punctuation errors, faulty verbs, incorrect usage.

The purpose of the technical writing stylebook is to help you understand the need for correctness and to instruct you in basic English grammar by using simple, easy-to-understand language designed for an uninitiated audience that knows very little or nothing about formal English grammar.

In addition to the instructions in the technical writing stylebook, you should have some other books handy for easy reference. Keep them on your desk and refer to them when you need them:

- Dictionary
- Thesaurus
- Synonyms and antonyms
- Style guides from professional societies in your technical field
- Style guides from industry in your technical field

4.0.2   Abbreviations

This is a list of commonly used technical abbreviations. Write the entire word the first time you use it and place the abbreviation in parentheses after it. Then you can abbreviate the word whenever you use it.

absolute	abs	cubic foot	cu ft
alkaline	alk	cubic inch	cu in
ampere	amp	cylinder	cyl
atmospheric	atm	degree	deg
atomic weight	at wt	diameter	diam
barometer	bar	efficiency	eff
board feet	bd ft	evaporate	evap
calorie	cal	feet per second	fps
candlepower	cp	foot	ft
centigram	cg		
chemical	chem	gallon	gal
conductivity	cond	gram	gm
cubic centimeter	cc	gravity	gr

horsepower	hp	number	no
inch	in	ounce	oz
insoluble	insol	pint	pt
kilocycle	kc	pound	lb
kilogram	kg	quart	qt
kilometer	km	revolutions per minute	rpm
kilowatt	kw	second	sec
liquid	liq	soluble	sol
lumen	lm	specific gravity	sp gr
maximum	max	temperature	temp
meter	m	viscosity	vix
miles per hour	mph	volt	V
millimeter	mm	weight	wt
minute	min	yard	yd
molecular weight	mol wt	year	yr

4.0.3 Capitalization

When you type your reports, use a capital letter only if you can justify it by one of the following rules. Rules for capitalization vary, but these are pretty standard.

- **Capitalize**

  •• Proper names and titles

  President John D. Rockefeller
  Dr. Ronald Jones
  Senator Cranston
  Dean of Students Rogers

  •• Words used to designate a particular part of the country

  the Northwest
  the East
  the South

  •• Names for the days of the week, months of the year, and holidays

  Monday
  June
  Memorial Day

•• The first word in a sentence

The case was closed.
He said, "The case was closed."

•• Important words in titles of books, articles, plays, films

"The Streets of San Francisco"
War and Peace
"One Day at a Time"

•• Names of countries and their languages

England, English
France, French
Holland, Dutch
Spain, Spanish

•• Names of states, rivers, places

California
American River
Mount Hood
Third Avenue and Forty-sixth Street

• **Do Not Capitalize**

•• Words for directions to geographic areas

I am going east on Highway 66.

The suspect headed north on Third and Townsend.

•• Names of seasons

It is spring, my favorite season of the year.

•• Titles when they are used as describers

Cranston is a senator from California

4.0.4 Correct Usage

Correct usage will sound professional and avoid noise in your reports. Remember that many people may read your reports, so it is important to write correctly.

• **Use Standard English.**

Be formal, but not stiff, and avoid management buzz words.

integrated	criteria	systems
inoperative	input	analysis

Use businesslike words, but not jargon, and avoid the overuse of *-ize* words.

> prioritize   finalize   weatherwise

Use the exact word, and avoid vague words.

> he said, <u>not</u> he indicated . . .
> she thought, <u>not</u> she assumed . . .

Use the simple, familiar word.

> draw, <u>not</u> delineate
> prevent, <u>not</u> obviate

• **Use the Right Word.**

Choose words from the spout of the funnel of words: the specific word.

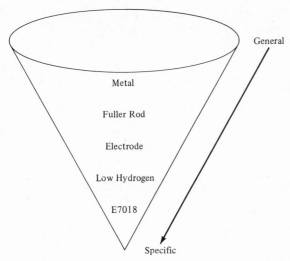

General

Metal

Fuller Rod

Electrode

Low Hydrogen

E7018

Specific

FIGURE 4.1

• **Use the Correct Pronoun.**

•• Subjective pronouns are *who, I, he, she, we, they.*

> <u>Who</u> is going to get the coffee?

> I am the one <u>who</u> is always first in line.

> It is <u>I</u> <u>who</u> am calling.

> The last one was <u>she</u>.

> The students are as smart as <u>they</u> (are).

•• Objective pronouns are *whom, me, him, her, them, us*

She is the candidate of <u>whom</u> we were thinking.

The president requested <u>us</u> officers to help cut costs.

Give the dividends to <u>them</u>.

He asked John and <u>me</u> to attend the meeting.

4.0.5 Numerals

Follow the general guidelines for decimals, fractions, and other uses.

• Decimals

Use a period and numerals to indicate decimal amounts; decimalization should not exceed two places in textual material unless there are special circumstances (1.25).

• Fractions

Spell out amounts less than one, using hyphens between the words (two-thirds, four-fifths); use figures for precise amounts larger than one, converting to decimals whenever possible ($1\frac{1}{2}$, 1.5); in tabular material, use figures exclusively.

• Other Uses

Always use figures for ages, addresses, aircraft names, centuries, channels, chapters, course numbers, dates, dimensions, distances, formulas, heights, model numbers, monetary units, page numbers, percentages, proportions, ratios, room numbers, serial numbers, sizes, telephone numbers, temperatures, years; for uses not covered by these listings, spell out whole numbers below 10, and use figures for 10 and above.

4.0.6 Parallel Structure

Parallel structure creates balance and clarifies and emphasizes ideas.

• Repeat the Grammatical Forms.

to clean	cleaning
to form	forming
to solder	soldering

The correct order of the operation is to clean, to form, and to solder.

The correct order of the operation is cleaning, forming, and soldering.

- **Balance the Grammatical Forms.**

    Engineering principles as well as architectural principles are taught in drafting classes.

    Not only piloting but also airframe maintenance is stressed in the aeronautics department.

4.0.7 Punctuation

Correct punctuation will avoid noise and help the reader see connections and separations.

- **Use a Comma to Show Separation of Items or Subordination of Ideas.**

  - Use a comma between items in a series of three or more.

    The secretary handled calls for the president, the vice-president, and the treasurer.

  - Use a comma before an *and* that makes two sentences into one.

    A maintenance man is now known as a maintenance person, and a secretary is now known as an administrative assistant.

  - Use a comma to separate interrupters.

    The other applicant, who is the one you interviewed, was not hired.

    Allen, in my opinion, is an outstanding applicant.

    "It is my decision," he said, "and I intend to stand by it."

  - Use a comma to show that something more important follows.

    Inasmuch as I was late for the meeting, I did not eat breakfast.

    Running through the parking lot, I dropped my purse.

  - Use a comma between coordinate (equal) elements that you can switch around.

    He is an attractive, well-dressed man.

    NOTE: When there are commas within the interrupters, set them apart with a dash at each end.

Three cities — Wayne, Morristown, and Nutley — are involved in the feasibility study.

• Use the Semicolon Only in the Following Situations.

•• Use the semicolon between items in a series of three or more if at least one item has a comma.

The tests were conducted by Paul Holmes, chief engineer; Wilson Pinney, supervisor; and Al Alexander, vice-president.

•• Use the semicolon before transitional (bridge) words such as *therefore, accordingly, consequently, furthermore, hence, moreover, nevertheless, then, thus.*

> **Warning** *Stop when you come to the end of a group of words that makes a sentence; use a semicolon or a period.*
> **Warning** *Make certain that a group of words forms a complete sentence before you stop, before you put in a semicolon or a period.*

Ordinary wear does not cause that amount of damage; therefore we have to look for another cause.

Engineer Thompson is doing an outstanding job; thus I recommend her for a promotion.

•• Use a semicolon between two groups of words connected by *and, but,* or *for* that could be made into two sentences if one group of words has commas within.

I am, therefore, very happy that a feasibility study is being done; and I hope it resolves the issue.

• Use a Colon Only in the Following Situations.

•• Use a colon to introduce a list at the end of a sentence.

The test results support the following data: too much stress on the wing, bolts made of inferior steel alloy, and cracks at the joints.

> **Warning** *Always place a colon after a noun or pronoun, not after the verb.*

•• Use a colon for other conventional uses: introducing long quotations, time, salutation on a business letter.

The list of items is as follows:
6:25
Dear Senator Cranston:

- **Use an Apostrophe Only in the Following Situations.**

•• Use an apostrophe plus *s* to form the singular possessive.

Martin's theory will not hold up under testing.

James's drawing shows the exact dimensions.

It is anybody's guess.

•• Use an apostrophe to form the plural possessive.

> **Warning** *Make certain that you form the plural of the word first; then put in the apostrophe.*

The girls' gym was out of bounds.

The Jameses' house was the scene of the company picnic.

Note that when the plural changes in spelling, you treat the possessive like a singular noun.

The women's room is on the first floor.

The men's gym is in the basement.

•• Use an apostrophe to form the plural of symbols, numbers, and letters of the alphabet.

The $\sqrt{}$'s are the problems in the calculations.

Be sure to check the statistics in the 1970's and 1980's.

The a's and the b's have already been alphabetized.

•• Use an apostrophe to show the omission of a letter.

It's going to be a very important contract.

I don't know if he'll be able to work on Friday.

> **Warning** *In general avoid contractions in report writing.*

- **Do Not Use an Apostrophe Within Possessive Pronouns.**

its		hers		theirs
	ours		yours	

4.0.8 Spell Correctly to Avoid Noise

Every time you write a report, you are judged by the reader. If you misspell words, your reader will think you do not take pride in your work. Incorrect spelling can ruin a good report.

You *can* spell correctly if you follow this helpful advice.

- **Consult the Dictionary.**

Sound out the word first, and then find it in the dictionary. Use the first or preferred spelling.

- **Consult the Official Technical Glossary or Stylebook in Your Technical Field.**

Words that are frequently used in your technical field will be listed in the stylebook.

- **Refer to a Few Simple Spelling Patterns.**

•• Use *i* before *e*
Except after *c*
Or when pronounced long *a*
As in *neighbor* and *weigh*.

Exceptions to memorize are *either, neither, leisure, seize, weird,* and *height.*

•• Drop the final *e*
when the ending begins
with a vowel: *a, e, i, o, u.*

```
curse     cursing
come      coming
write     writing
```

Exceptions arise when you want to keep the hard *g* or a soft *c*.

```
courage   courageous
notice    noticeable
```

•• Keep the final *e*
when the ending begins with a consonant (all other letters of the alphabet).

```
live      lively
nine      ninety
love      lovely
```

Exceptions are these:

```
true      truly
nine      ninth
```

•• Change *y* to *i*
when *y* is preceded by a consonant.

gully   gullies
apply   applied

•• Do not change *y* to *i*
when *y* is preceded by a vowel.

pay   pays
attorney attorneys

•• Double the final consonant
when it is preceded by a single vowel

pen   penned
blot   blotted

and when the accent is on the last syllable.

omit   omitted
begin   beginning

•• Do not double the final consonant
when the final consonant is preceded by two vowels

despair   despairing
leer   leering

and when the accent is on the first syllable of the modified word.

benefit   benefited
prefer   preference

• **Refer to Spelling List.**

The following is a list of words technical writers often misspell. It is a good idea to memorize words you consistently misspell.

acceptable	align	bylaw	channel
accessible	allotted		citywide
accommodate	all right	calendar	clear-cut
achievement	analysis	cancel	clientele
acknowledgment	analyze	cancellation	collateral
addressed	appropriate	capital	commitment
adjustment	assurance	capitol	compatible
administration	authorize	carry-over	competitor
advisable		catalog	concession
advisory	beneficial	Celsius	conscientious
afterward	bona fide	centigrade	consensus
aggravate	boundary	changeable	controlled
airtight	brand-new	changeover	council

counsel
criteria

deductible
deferred
deficiency
depreciation
desirable
deterrent
discrepancy
discriminate
dissatisfied
dissociate

eligible
enterprise
entrepreneur
environment
equipped
equivalent
exaggerate

fact-finding
feasible
forfeit
fulfill

gauge
government
grievance
guarantee

hand-picked
horsepower

illusion
immaterial
implement
inasmuch as
incur
indispensable
innovation
integrate

judgment

kilocycles
kilometer
know-how

laboratory
lawsuit
liability
liaison

maintenance
manageable
memorandum
merchandise
middleman
minuscule
miscellaneous
mock-up
moneymaker

necessary
negligence

negligible
noticeable

obsolete
occurred
omission
one-sided
optimistic

parallel
particle
percent
permissible
personnel
pertinent
phenomenon
pipeline
policy-maker
practical
predominant
preferred
principal
principle
privilege
procedure
profit-sharing

quasar
questionnaire

receipt
recommendation
referred
reimburse

relevant
respectfully
rhythm

satellite
semiannual
separate
serviceable
sizable
spacecraft
species
sponsor
stockbroker
subsidiary
successor
supersonic
syllabus

telecast
thorough
titleholder
transferred

undoubtedly

vacuum
vice-president
videotape

warrant
week-long
wholly
workday
worn-out

4.0.9 Verbs

To make certain that you say what you intended to, you must use verbs correctly.

• Use Active Verbs.

Active verbs will make your writing more forceful as they eliminate many unneeded words.

The supervisor <u>wants</u> an immediate report.

Engineering <u>checked</u> the blueprints.

Note how passive verbs slow down your forcefulness.

An immediate report <u>was wanted</u> by the supervisor.

The blueprints <u>were checked</u> by engineering.

- **Use the Present Tense**

- to define terms,

    A diode is a device that lets electric current flow through in one direction only.

- to state a theory or a proposition,

    We propose an environmental impact study before we start on plans for the widening of Willow Road.

- to give instructions,

    Before you leave, turn off the switch.

- and to describe a mechanism.

    A meter box is a useful device.

- **Use the Command Form**

- to give instructions.

    <u>Replace</u> all laboratory equipment before you leave and <u>turn</u> off the lights.

- **Make Subjects and Verbs Agree in Number.**

If the subject of the sentence is singular, the verb must be singular in number. Do not let any group of words between the subject and verb get in the way.

The <u>list</u> of instructions that came with the camera <u>is</u> in the case.

- **Use a Singular Verb.**

- When the subject is *each, everyone, everybody, either, neither, anybody, somebody.*

    <u>Each</u> of the applicants <u>has</u> a good chance of being hired by the department.

Either is applicable to the case.

- •• When the subject is time, money, or measurement.

  Five thousand two hundred and eighty feet is the number of feet in a mile.

  Five years is the time we estimate for the job.

  Ten million dollars is the estimated cost of the new prison.

- • **Use the Correct Tense of Confusing Verbs (lie/lay, sit/set, rise/raise).**

- •• *To lie* is a verb meaning to recline.

  Today I lie down.

  Yesterday I lay down.

  I have lain down.

- •• *To lay* is a verb meaning to place.

  Today I lay the calculator on the desk.

  Yesterday I laid the calculator on the desk.

  I have laid the calculator on the desk.

- •• *To sit* is a verb meaning to recline.

  Today I sit at my desk.

  Yesterday I sat at my desk.

  I have sat at my desk.

- •• *To set* is a verb meaning to place.

  Today I set the calculator on the desk.

  Yesterday I set the calculator on the desk.

  I have set the calculator on the desk.

- •• *To rise* is a verb meaning to get up.

  Today I rise at 8:00 A.M.

  Yesterday I rose at 8:00 A.M.

  I have risen at 8:00 A.M. all week.

- •• *To raise* is a verb meaning to lift up.

  Today I raise the blinds.

Yesterday I raised the blinds.

I have raised the blinds.

• Use the Correct Meaning of Confusing Verbs (affect/effect, to hang, let/leave, can/may).

•• *To affect* is a verb meaning "to influence," "to imitate," "to move emotionally."

Lack of sleep affects [influences] your reaction.

She affected [imitated] a British dialect.

The president was affected [moved emotionally] by his wife's death.

•• *To effect* is a verb meaning to bring about.

The drug effected [brought about] a cure.

•• *Effect* used as a noun means "the result."

The effect [result] of the drug is hallucinatory.

•• *To hang* is a verb meaning "to suspend with a rope around the neck until dead" or "to attach," "to fasten," or "to support."

Today the prisoner hanged himself with his belt.

Yesterday the prisoner hanged himself with his belt.

The prisoner has hanged himself with his belt.

Today I hang the wallpaper.

Yesterday I hung the wallpaper.

I have hung the wallpaper.

•• *To let* is a verb meaning "to allow" or "to permit." *To leave* is a verb meaning "to depart."

Let me have the day off to go to the doctor.

Leave us because we want to be alone.

•• *Can* is a verb used to express ability to perform. *May* is a verb used to request permission or to show uncertainty.

Richards can take shorthand with great speed.

May she take the exam for administrative assistant?

She may apply for the job.

4.10   Use the Correct Vocabulary.

Incorrect
- Being as he was ill . . .
- Due to the rate of inflation . . .
- She is different than me.
- These kind of jobs . . .
- Those kind of reports . . .
- Less persons are employed here.
- Most all the staff are here.
- The engineer is different than me.
- He is different than me.
- She is real accurate.
- Susan is doing good.
- He should of been here.
- Try and pick up the groceries.
- His belt is lose.
- The principle cause of absence . . .
- Weather or not we get promoted . . .
- The boss complemented him.
- I feel badly.
- Running through the woods, the trees looked beautiful.

Correct
- Because he was ill . . .
- Because of the rate of inflation . . .
- She is different from me.
- These kinds of jobs . . .
- Those kinds of reports . . .
- Fewer persons are employed here.
- Almost all the staff are here.
- The engineer is different from me.
- He is different than I [am].
- She is really [or very] accurate.
- Susan is doing well.
- He should have been here.
- Try to pick up the groceries.
- His belt is loose.
- The principal cause of absence . . .
- Whether or not we get promoted . . .
- The boss complimented him.
- I feel bad.
- Running through the woods, I saw some beautiful trees.

List other vocabulary words you may think of that are used incorrectly and correct them:

Incorrect
-
-
-
-
-
-
-
-
-
-

Correct
-
-
-
-
-
-
-
-
-
-

- **Divide Words Correctly.**

When you reach the end of a line and have to carry part of a word over to the next line, break it between syllables and place a hyphen at the end of the line.

> He was not able to discrim-
> inate between red and yellow.

Warning *Check your dictionary for syllable division of words, for example,* dis · crim · i · na · tion.

- **Avoid Wordiness.**

                    unnecessary
Eliminate all ∧ words ~~that are unnecessary~~.

> The supervisor repeated his orders ~~again~~.
>
>   to
> President Gomez arrived early ~~so that he could~~ ∧ check the figures.
>
> The 757, ~~which is~~ a more efficient fuel saver, is being adopted by our company for short runs.
>
> Supervisor Campbell, ~~who is~~ a competent woman, is in charge of the department.

Where You Have Been

You have some simple instructions for capitalization, usage, numerals, parallel structure, punctuation, spelling, verbs, and vocabulary.

If you are not certain of how to write something, look it up in the technical writing stylebook, your dictionary, your thesaurus, or your antonym and synonym book.

Write simply, write clearly, write concisely, write correctly.

And revise, revise, revise, revise.

Exercises

Rewrite the following sentences and make them clear and concise.

1. Due to the fact that Smith did not have seniority, it was indicated by Supervisor Johnson that he would not be promoted.

_____

_____

_____

2. The shuttle will go Thursday unless there are unforeseen problems we do not know about.

_____

_____

_____

3. At this point in time the project is finalized and experiments to record specific research quality data are indicated.

_____

_____

_____

4. Weatherwise we can finalize our flight plan and take off on time.

_____

_____

_____

5. The correct order of operations is to file the flight plan, do a routine check on the plane, and asking the tower for instructions.

_____

_____

_____

6. Being as it is a very busy day, the plant engineer indicated that it seemed necessary to prioritize the workload.

_____

_____

_____

7. Prior to this event Marshall assumed that he would be contacted and the office would indicate that he was up for promotion.

_____

_____

_____

8. The bottom line is profitability which is maximized by superior output by employees on all levels.

_____

_____

_____

9. The draftsperson delineated the plans for the generator capacitor in the event that we have a blackout.

_____

_____

_____

10. It is our belief that in view of the fact that the comptroller acted in a hasty manner, the company fired employees unnecessarily.

_____

_____

_____

Circle the correct pronoun.

11. I checked (he, him) in at noon.

12. The supervisor gave (we, us) technicians a special assignment.

13. The plant engineer asked (we, us) technicians to revise our reports.

14. The other drivers were going faster than (I, me) at the time of the accident.

15. Nobody except (he, him) thanked us for our cooperation.

16. (Who, Whom) did you see on your way to work?

17. (Who, Whom) do you think will be appointed to the job?

18. The in-house memo is for you and (I, me).

19. (Who, Whom) is on the phone?

20. It is (she, her).

Circle the correct verb.

21. The pamphlet was (laying, lying) on the shelf.

22. I went home and (lay, laid) down.

23. You can (lay, lie) the report on the desk.

24. The secretary can't (accept, except) the call.

25. I was able to (sit, set) down and write my report this morning.

26. My eyes were (effected, affected) by the drug.

27. The carpenter (hanged, hung) the rafters in the dining room.

28. (Let, Leave) me have my locker key.

29. (Can, May) Johnson take the afternoon off?

30. (Lay, Lie) low until you are called on.

31. She had a headache and has (laid, lain) down all afternoon.

32. Frank was hurt badly in the shop and (may, can) never walk again.

Punctuate and capitalize the following sentences.

33. The contract was signed on friday april 9 1982 and notarized at once

34. Employees who go back to school and earn ba degrees ma degrees and phd degrees will receive incentive pay

35. Because the parking lot was filled to capacity I had to park on the street

36. The applicant he thought was too inexperienced for the job

37. The personnel manager however did not want to discourage the applicant

38. The application the personnel interviewer stated could have been more correctly completed

39. The report is completed however if we need to rewrite it we shall do so

40. The salaries should be negotiated on the following items sick leave cost of living raises insurance benefits working conditions etc

41. The package was delivered in good condition however there was money due for postage

42. Take a turn on the social committee and come to the meeting at the mens gym on thirty sixth street and lexington avenue

43. The exit signs in the department are well marked like ours

44. The womens volley ball game will be held at James house

45. Charles said I have to deposit a check at the bank of new york because im overdrawn

Circle the correct word.

46. Marge had (all ready, already) checked out the new employee.

47. The report (dosen't, doesn't) look very attractive or easy to read.

48. He will not (accept, except) the offer.

49. The (attornies, attorneys) drew up the contract.

50. The night watchman is (truly, truely) a brave person.

51. The supervisor's order had a (noticeable, noticable) effect on morale.

52. Because he was an excellent (writer, writter), he was given a desk job.

53. The report was (alright, all right) the way it was written.

54. I hope the students (benefited, benefitted) from these exercises.

APPENDIX A
Looking for a Job

Job Investigation

1.0.1   Preparation

Make an inventory of your interests, education, experience, and skills.
Write an autobiography that includes the following items:

1. Look at the things you have succeeded in and enjoyed the most.
2. Decide whether you relate best to people or to things.
3. Decide whether you find the most satisfaction in stability or in change.
4. Decide whether you are willing to travel anywhere in the world for a job.
5. Decide whether you work better alone or with people.
6. Think about the skills and experience you have that will make you attractive to a potential employer.

1.0.2   Plan Ahead for the Job Interview.

Remember that you are selling yourself.

1. Be positive about why you want to work for that company.
2. Be neat and well groomed.
3. Be friendly and relaxed but not overly casual.
4. Be more interested in the work involved on the job and its potential for future advancement than in the fringe benefits.
5. Know what your skills are, what you are good at, and what you want to do for that company.
6. Know how long the company has been in existence and about any of its accomplishments.
7. Sound positive when answering questions.

Q: What do you like least?
A: I don't like it when I do less than excellent work.

Q: What do you like best?
A: When I do the best job I'm capable of doing.

Q: What is your greatest fear?
A: That I won't live up to my own expectations.

Role play the job interview.

1. Tell me something about yourself.
2. Why do you want to work for this company?

3. Do you enjoy (   ) work?
4. Why have you chosen this field for your vocation?
5. How do you see yourself 10 years from now?
6. What skills do you have that could be of benefit to us?
7. Are you able to take criticism?
8. What are your strong points?
9. What are your weak points?
10. Do you feel that you are loyal?
11. What were your responsibilities in your last job?
12. What were your favorite subjects in school?
13. What are some of your interests or hobbies outside of work?

1.0.3   Reasons Given for Not Hiring

The following have been given by company personnel officers as their reason for not hiring an applicant for a job.

1. Too passive
2. Ill at ease
3. Never heard of company
4. Personal appearance
5. Overbearing
6. Poor voice
7. Overemphasis on money
8. Poor scholastic record

1.0.4   Things to Do and to Avoid in a Job Interview

This is a compilation of many helpful suggestions from personnel people.

1. Be open and straightforward.
2. Do not give a "dead fish" handshake.
3. Do not discuss your friction with your parents.
4. Do not say that your parents make all the decisions.
5. Do not talk about contacts (pull) in the company.
6. Do not be cynical.
7. Do not show your inability to take criticism.
8. Do not spout radical ideas.
9. Do not be late for an interview.

10. If you are asked if you have any questions, respond definitely by asking a question, for example, "Do the employees in your department work together on group projects?"

Warning   *The cutting edge is skills that are transferable from one job to another:*

> Punctuality,
> Dependability,
> Caring,
> Excellence.

1.0.5   Have a Job Plan.

Remember that if you are going to spend 40 hours a week at a job, you ought to have a job plan.

> What do I want to do? (What are the skills I enjoy the most?)
> Where do I want to do it?
> For whom do I want to work?
> How will I get the job?

Interview key personnel, friends, and relatives; write résumés; fill out applications; answer ads.

Letter of Application

1.0.6   Sell Yourself.

The content will change as you change and add educational and work experience.

The format should remain the same.

There should be three or four paragraphs on one sheet of paper.

Paragraph *one* is the point of contact.

Say where or how you heard of the job.

Paragraphs *two* and *three* are the sales pitch.

Tell how you are different from other applicants.

State what you have that is a marketable skill or advantage.

Ask your reader to please refer to your résumé.

Paragraph *four* is a request for an interview at the convenience of the receiver of the letter. A good suggestion is to follow up with a telephone call one week later.

State specifically when you can be reached by phone.

1255 El Cerrito Avenue
San Mateo, California 94022
15 November 198_

Ms. Esmey Mills
Personnel Manager
Hewlitt-Damion Company
20 Data Road
Fosdick, California 94072

Dear Ms. Mills:

Last month our drafting club at the College of San Mateo had the privilege of touring your plant. I was very impressed with the work that you are doing in the field of electronics and feel a strong desire to work for your company, the leader in the electronics field.

I would like to apply for a position of junior draftsperson in your design department. My advisor, Dennis Stack, at the College of San Mateo, told me that this position will be open on December 1.

Mr. Stack has helped me select course work that should be valuable in the field of electronics as well as in drafting. For example, I have taken courses in electronics circuitry as well as in machine shop welding in addition to my drafting technology courses. Elective courses in technical writing and public speaking add another dimension to my skills.

I would appreciate an interview at your convenience. I can be reached at (415) 395-1978 between 8:00 and 10:00 a.m.

Sincerely,

Evelyn Stewart Carter

Evelyn Stewart Carter

Résumé enclosed

A Résumé

1.0.7 Be Brief.

Use one-page format. (As employment and responsibilities increase, the
job description may take more than one page.)
Leave lots of white space.
Have the résumé professionally typed.
Reproduce as many copies as needed.

1.0.8 Be Forceful.

List name, address, and phone number.
State job objective.
List education (present to past).
List experience (present to past).

1.0.9 Write "References on Request" (at bottom left).

EVELYN STEWART CARTER

1255 El Cerrito Avenue
San Mateo, California 94022   (415) 395-1978

JOB OBJECTIVE: Draftsperson
- -

Education   College of San Mateo

Candidate for Associate of Science degree in
June 1984.

Major in drafting technology with emphasis on
reading drawings and sketches of architectural
plans and electronics schematics; completed
course in technical writing in addition to
required general education courses plus major.

Graduated from San Mateo High School in the
upper 10 percent of class in June 1982.

Experience

1982   PARKER PRECISION CO.
to
Present   Working 30 hours a week as drafting
apprentice doing electronics schematics. The
job includes reading engineering specifications
and drawings.

1979   HABER HI-FI, SAN MATEO, CALIFORNIA
to
1982   Worked 25 hours a week as salesperson selling
all types of radio and electronic equipment.
This involved explaining, demonstrating,
giving instructions for operating equipment.

References on request.

APPENDIX B
Sample Student Papers

CARBON-COMPOSITION RESISTOR

1.0 INTRODUCTION

A carbon-composition resistor consists of a resistive element, axial leads, a plastic case, and four color-coded bands. A resistor is an element used to reduce supply voltages to some desired value or to limit current. Resistors are used in most familiar electrical appliances and devices.

2.0 PARTS IN DETAIL

A resistive element, axial leads, a plastic case, and four color-coded bands make up the most popular and inexpensive resistors. (Refer to Figure 1.)

2.1 List of Parts

1. Resistive element

2. Axial leads

3. Plastic case

4. Four color-coded bands

1

Solid
Resistance Element

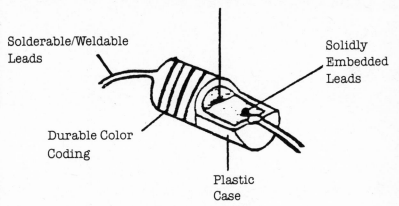

Solderable/Weldable
Leads

Solidly
Embedded
Leads

Durable Color
Coding

Plastic
Case

Figure 1   Carbon-Composition Resistor

2.2   Detailed Description

2.2.1   Resistive Element

The resistive element is a composition of carbon particles and a binding resin; the proportions are varied to provide the desired resistance.

2.2.2   Axial Leads

Attached to the ends of the resistive element are axial leads of tinned copper wire for soldering the resistor into a circuit.

2

2.2.3 Plastic Case

The plastic case surrounds the unit to prevent
moisture and other harmful elements from entering.
(Angerbauer:29)

2.2.4 Color Bands

Four color-coded bands are painted around the
resistor body near one end. The color bands identify the
resistive value of the resistor. (See Table 1.)

TABLE 1 Carbon Resistor Color Code

	1st Band	2nd Band	No. Zeros or Multiply by	Tolerance (%)
Black	0	0	0	
Brown	1	1	1	
Red	2	2	2	
Orange	3	3	3	
Yellow	4	4	4	
Green	5	5	5	
Blue	6	6	6	
Violet	7	7	7	
Gray	8	8	8	
White	9	9	9	
Gold	—	—	0.1	5
Silver	—	—	0.01	10
No color	—	—	—	20

3.0 SUMMARY

A resistor is a simple element used in electrical devices to reduce supply voltages or to limit current to some desired value. Carbon-composition resistors are the most popular of all resistors because they are inexpensive and effective for most applications. They are composed of a carbon resistive element enclosed in a plastic case. Axial leads at each end of the resistor are used for soldering into a circuit. Four color-coded bands are painted around one end of the resistor to show their resistive value.

THE VALVE TRAIN

1.0 INTRODUCTION

The valve train is a series of parts in the engine of a plane that allows internal combustion to take place. The valve train consists of a camshaft, tappet, push rod, rocker arm, valve spring, exhaust valve, and intake valve.

2.0 PARTS IN DETAIL

The camshaft, tappet, push rod, rocker arm, valve spring, and exhaust and intake valves are the main parts of the valve train. Each performs a specific job. (Fig. 1)

2.1 List of Parts

1. Camshaft

2. Tappet

3. Push rod

4. Rocker arm

5. Valve spring

6. Exhaust valve

7. Intake valve

1

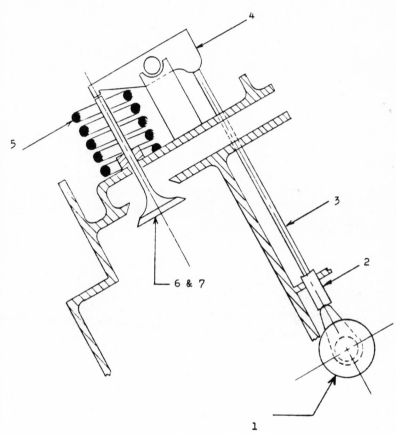

Figure 1   Valve Train

2.2   Detailed Description

2.2.1   Camshaft

The camshaft is made of cast iron and has a machined surface 24 inches in length with four 1-inch diameter main bearings and 16 lobes. The camshaft is the driving force behind the valve train.

2.2.2   Tappet

The tappet is constructed of solid hardened carbon steel and is .50 inch in diameter and 1.25 inches long. The tappet rides on the camshaft lobe. The tappet's main function is to push the rod leading into the rocker arm.

2.2.3   Push Rod

The push rod is approximately 8 inches long by .25 inch in diameter and is made of hardened carbon steel. The push rod rides on the tappet and is connected to the rocker arm. The push rod transfers the upward lift of the cam and tappet to the upper valve assembly.

3

2.2.4 Rocker Arm

The rocker arm is made of forged and hardened carbon steel and is approximately 3 inches by .50 inch. The rocker arm is the recipient of the push rod's upward motion. The rocker arm transfers upward motion of the cam lobe and presses down on the valve spring.

2.2.5 Valve Spring

The valve spring, constructed of hardened spring steel, is 3 inches long and has a 1.25-inch diameter. The spring is secured to the valve by valve keepers. The spring simply returns the valve to the valve seat in the closed position.

2.2.6 Intake Valve

The intake valve is made of high-speed machined steel and is 6 inches long with a flange of 1.375 inches. The valve is filled with sodium. The sodium adds cooling properties to the valve at high-temperature operating speeds. The intake valve is smaller than the exhaust valve.

4

2.2.7 Exhaust Valve

The exhaust valve is constructed of the same materials as the intake valve but is .625 inches larger. The exhaust valve opens and allows compression to expel burned-up fuel from the combustion chamber.

3.0 SUMMARY

The valve train is a series of parts which are designed to open and close valves on an internal combustion engine. The camshaft, tappet, push rod, rocker arm, valve spring, and intake and exhaust valves all contribute to the internal combustion process of the plane engine.

WRITING AN INSTRUCTION MANUAL

1.0 INTRODUCTION

A documentation specialist in the computer field must write and revise instruction manuals for departments that are responsible for providing input to the computer. To do this, the specialist studies any existing documentation and conducts interviews with the department clerks. First notes are taken in instruction form, incorporated with existing documentation, and bound together. This material is revised by the department supervisor and the computer department supervisor. When approved the documentation is printed, bound, and distributed to all concerned personnel for a trial period. Relevant suggestions are then added, and the manual is designated complete.

These are some definitions which may be helpful:

Documentation includes forms, instructions, notes, and illustrations in one category.

Input encompasses both the reading of information into the computer and the information itself.

1

2.0 STEPS IN DETAIL

Writing an Instruction Manual includes these steps: Existing documentation is studied; the current instructions are written from this information and then revised by the department supervisor and the computer department supervisor; instructions are printed, bound, and distributed; suggestions and revisions are incorporated into the manual and distributed for a trial period before it is designated complete and used exclusively in training new personnel. (See Figure 1.)

2.1 List of Steps

1. Existing documentation studied

2. Interviews held with department clerks

3. Documentation revised

4. Manuals printed, bound, and distributed

5. Trial period designated

6. Manual designated complete

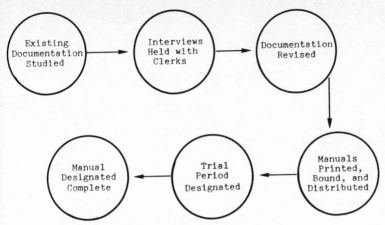

Figure 1　Writing an Instruction Manual

2.2　Detailed Description

2.2.1　Existing Documentation Studied

There are several types of forms used for the input

of different types of information. These forms are

photocopied and are placed in the instruction manual.

Any written instructions currently used are also studied.

2.2.2　Interviews Held with Department Clerks

After obtaining clearance from the department

supervisor, interviews are scheduled with the department

clerks. Copies of any forms and written instructions are

brought to the meeting. These help to determine the current information flow. Notes are taken and instructions are written from these notes outlining how to complete the forms and where to get the information to do so. These instructions are reviewed by the department clerks to ensure accuracy.

2.2.3   Documentation Revised

The documentation is amended by the department supervisor and the computer department supervisor. Suggestions by the department supervisor may provide overall insight not obtainable from the clerks. Suggestions by the computer department may include revision of the current forms used. Any suggestions are incorporated into the instructions.

2.2.4   Instructions Printed, Bound, and Distributed

The instructions are printed and then bound together with the sample forms into manuals.

These are distributed to the department clerks, the department supervisor, and the computer department file.

2.2.5 Trial Period Designated

The trial period elicits suggestions which evolve from the actual use of the manuals. Some of these suggestions may involve the clarification of the instructions or revision of a form. Amendments are sent as supplements to manual holders.

2.2.6 Manual Designated Complete

After the trial period the manual is designated complete. The manuals are used to train personnel within the departments and to provide information to the computer department. Major changes in the computer system or the department system can be made smoother when a base of information, such as the manual, is provided.

3.0 SUMMARY

The instruction manuals are used to familiarize personnel with the forms and procedures within a department. The computer system provides reports only as accurate as the information input. This method of instruction must therefore train personnel to provide

5

consistently accurate input. The instruction manuals are

developed from the department's input forms together

with instructions based on the department's current

process. Revision by both the department supervisor and

the computer department supervisor is essential to avoid

basic errors in instructions or forms. After being

printed, bound, and distributed the manuals are contin-

ually reviewed until major change makes them obsolete.

JET ENGINE MAINTENANCE PROCESS

1.0 INTRODUCTION

Jet engine maintenance is a process which systematically keeps commercial jet engines in serviceable condition. The engine is removed from an aircraft, reviewed and inspected by technical maintenance personnel, disassembled, assembled, tested and inspected, made serviceable, and installed on an aircraft.

Here are some definitions which will help you understand this process:

An A.D. note is an Airworthiness Directive issued by the Federal Aviation Administration requiring a mandatory change for safety reasons. This is similar to having your car recalled by the manufacturer.

Cause is a general maintenance problem such as high oil consumption. It is similar to replacing a light bulb in your home.

Hard-time limit is the maximum time limit allowed by the manufacturer before a part has to be replaced. This is similar to an official elected for a designated term of office.

A module is a complete assembly of parts. A front and rear compressor, front and rear turbine, hot section, intermediate case, and exhaust case are all modules. A burner is to a stove as a module is to an engine.

A test cell is a soundproof room with 12-inch thick cement walls. Inside the cell, the engine is connected to a series of tubes and wires which connect to a control room similar to a cockpit. The engine is run at flight speeds, and all repairs are tested. The test is the same as the test drive your auto mechanic gives your car before you pay the bill.

2.0 STEPS IN DETAIL

After removal from an aircraft, the engine is reviewed and inspected, disassembled, assembled, tested, inspected, made serviceable, and installed on the aircraft.

2

2.1   <u>List of Steps</u> (See Figure 1.)

1. Removal

2. Review and inspection

3. Disassembly

4. Assembly

5. Test, inspection, and serviceability

6. Installation

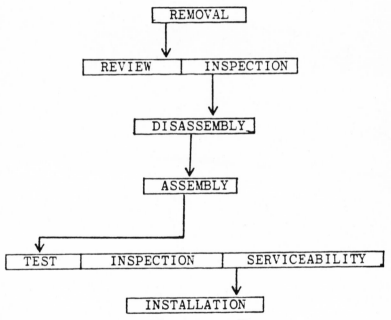

Figure 1   Jet Engine Maintenance Process

3

2.2 Detailed Description

2.2.1 Removal of Engine

For various reasons an engine is removed from an aircraft: hard-time limits, A.D. note, cause, or work-load scheduling. An engine stand, hoist, and manpower are used to remove the engine. The job takes approximately $2\frac{1}{2}$ hours.

2.2.2 Review and Inspection

The engine is received at the maintenance facility and is assigned to a stall. Extensive tracking and documentation begins. A meeting is held by a repair foreman, engineer, production planner, review inspector, and maintenance specialist who mutually decide what is to be accomplished during the shop visit.

2.2.3 Disassembly

Manpower is assigned to disassemble the engine. It is broken down into modules that are routed to

4

various back shops for rework, inspection, and replacement of parts.

2.2.4 Assembly

After the rework and replacement process, the modules are routed back to the stall. The mechanics assemble the modules into a complete engine.

2.2.5 Test, Inspection, Serviceability

The engine is moved to a test cell and a full engine run is performed. If the test is successful, an airframe and powerplant licensed inspector declares the engine airworthy and tags it serviceable.

2.2.6 Installation

The engine is routed by truck or tug from the maintenance facility back to an aircraft. It is installed with an engine stand, hoist, and manpower, a process that takes approximately $3\frac{1}{2}$ hours.

5

3.0 SUMMARY

The process of maintaining a jet engine is a complex, systematic series of events which includes removal, review, inspection, disassembly, assembly, test, inspection, serviceability, and installation. Technical engine maintenance personnel use this process to maintain engine reliability and professionalism in commercial aviation.

INSTRUCTIONS FOR SECOND-SHIFT INPUT OPERATORS

1.0 INTRODUCTION

Input operators who work the second shift should observe the following instructions closely. First, check in with the shift operator and log in the job assigned to you. Then review any previous work. Continue the work until the job is complete, log in the completion of the job, and return the input sheets to the shift operator. Then obtain your next assignment. These steps are to be followed in the specified order by all input operators.

2.0 STEPS IN DETAIL

2.1 List of Steps

1. Check in with the shift operator.

2. Log in the job assignment.

3. Review previous work.

4. Work until completion.

5. Log in the job's completion.

6. Return input sheets to the shift operator.

7. Obtain the next job assignment.

TABLE 1   Sample Log Book

Job Number	Priority Number	Name of Operator	Time Begun	Time Completed	Operator's Initials
302	1	J. Moore	9:05	9:35	J. M.
703	3	S. Same	9:07	9:15	S. S.

2.2   Detailed Description

2.2.1   Check in with the Shift Operator.

Check in with the shift operator for your job assignment. If there is a job with high priority, it will be assigned to you. If there are none more critical, a job that the first shift was unable to complete will be assigned to you.

2.2.2   Log in the Job Assignment.

After the shift operator allots the assignment to you, log it in. Take the log book and list the job number, its priority number, your name, and the time.

2.2.3   Review Previous Work.

If the job has not been completed by the first shift, review the input sheets to see where the operator had left off. Inquire to assure the mode used had been balanced properly before being shut off.

2.2.4   Work Until Completion.

Work until the job assignment has been completed. Make sure the job properly balances and you correctly sign out of the mode used. If there is a request for a copy of a report on your input, run off the information requested and return it to the shift operator.

2.2.5   Log in the Job's Completion.

Log in the job's completion. Locate the original point
you logged in and complete the line. To do this, list the time
the job was completed and sign your initials.

2.2.6   Return Input Sheets to the Shift Operator.

Return the input sheets completed and any reports to
the shift operator. Make sure the input sheets are properly
bound together and are in the correct sequence.

2.2.7   Obtain the Next Job Assignment.

Obtain the next job assignment from the shift operator.
Follow the same procedure as for the first assignment and
continue until your break or the end of your shift.

3.0   SUMMARY

The second-shift input operator first checks in with
the shift operator for the job assignment and logs in
this assignment. Then he or she reviews any incomplete
input, works until it is complete and logs the completion of the job. He or she returns the input to the

shift operator and receives his or her next assignment.

This procedure was established to assure the smooth

flow of work and to ensure the security of the input

documents. This system enables the location of all input

in the computer department at any specified time.

INSTRUCTIONS FOR USING OHM'S LAW
TO CALCULATE CURRENT

1.0 INTRODUCTION

Ohm's law shows the relationship among voltage, resistance, and current in an electrical circuit. Current in an electric circuit is proportional to the applied voltage and inversely proportional to its resistance; therefore to solve for current, divide voltage by resistance; to solve for resistance, divide voltage by current; and to solve for voltage, multiply current by resistance. (Angerbauer:69-81) With an understanding of Ohm's law, technicians will be able to calculate the current in a circuit with a given applied voltage and resistance.

You will need to know the following definitions:

<u>Electric current</u> (I), measured in amperes (A), is a flow of electrons through a conductor or device. (Angerbauer:15)

<u>Electromotive force</u> (E) is the force of pressure resulting from a potential difference. (Angerbauer:13)

1

<u>Potential difference</u> is the excess or lack of electrons at one point compared to the excess or lack of electrons at some other point. (Angerbauer:11)

<u>Resistance</u> (R), measured in ohms (Ω), is the opposition which a material or device offers to electric current. (Angerbauer:17)

Voltage (V or E) is the unit of measurement that has been derived to express potential difference. (Angerbauer:13)

2.0 STEPS IN DETAIL

To solve for current, divide voltage by resistance; to solve for resistance, divide voltage by current; and to solve for voltage, multiply current by resistance.

2.1 <u>List of Steps</u>

1. Solve for current.

2. Solve for resistance.

3. Solve for voltage.

TABLE 1   Ohm's Law Formulas

Formulas for determining unknown values of . . .			
Known Values	I	R	E
I & R			IR
I & E		$\dfrac{E}{I}$	
R & E	$\dfrac{E}{R}$		

(Bertini:121)

2.2   Detailed Description

2.2.1   Solve for Current (I).

Divide voltage by resistance to solve for current in a circuit when voltage and resistance are known. (See Table 1.) Find the current in Figure 1.

$$I = \frac{E}{R}$$

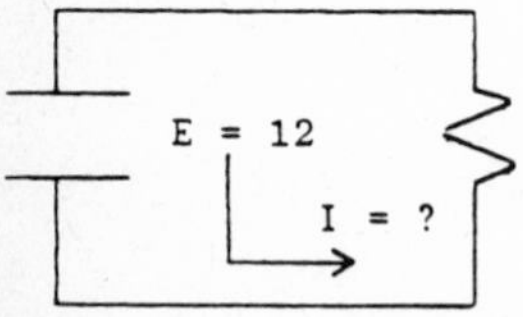

$R = 3$ Substitute values:

$$I = \frac{12}{3} \qquad I = 4$$

Figure 1   Schematic of Simple Circuit

2.2.2 Solve for Resistance (R).

Divide voltage by current to solve for resistance in a circuit when voltage and current are known. (See Table 1.) Find the resistance in Figure 2.

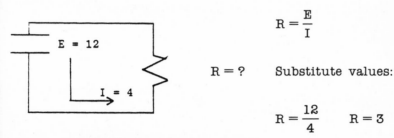

$$R = \frac{E}{I}$$

R = ?   Substitute values:

$$R = \frac{12}{4} \qquad R = 3$$

Figure 2 Schematic of Simple Circuit

2.2.3 Solve for Voltage (E).

Multiply current by resistance to solve for voltage in a circuit when current and resistance are known. (See Table 1.) Find voltage in Figure 3.

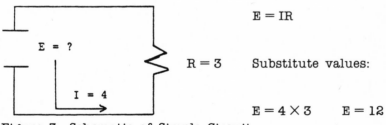

$$E = IR$$

R = 3   Substitute values:

$$E = 4 \times 3 \qquad E = 12$$

Figure 3 Schematic of Simple Circuit

4

3.0 SUMMARY

It is necessary for electronics technicians to be able to calculate current, voltage, and resistance in a circuit. Current in an electric circuit is proportional to the applied voltage and inversely proportional to its resistance; therefore to solve for current, divide voltage by resistance $\left(I = \dfrac{E}{R}\right)$; to solve for resistance, divide voltage by current $\left(R = \dfrac{E}{I}\right)$; and to solve for voltage, multiply current by resistance $(E = IR)$.

BIBLIOGRAPHY

Angerbauer, George J. Principles of DC and AC Circuits. New York: Breton Publishers, 1978.

Bertini, Tullio. Learning Modules in Passive Circuits and Devices. San Mateo, Cal.: College of San Mateo, 1981.

6

MEMORANDUM

TO: Robert Newell, Instructor	DATE: 13 November 19
FROM: Ron Scheldrup, Student	
PURPOSE: Progress Report on Term Project for ET-380	

This is to advise you that my term project, which is an electronic star chart, is being completed on schedule according to our contract. I foresee no problems in having the system completed on time.

We signed a contract on 25 September 198_ stating which steps I will have completed by when. The contract stated that there will be four intermediate checkpoints and a final evaluation. The first and second evaluations have already occurred (on 8 October and 30 October respectively). The third evaluation will occur during the week of 23 to 25 November, the fourth will be between 14 and 18 December, and the final evaluation will occur between 11 and 15 January 198_. (See Table 1.)

1

TABLE 1   Term Project Completion Schedule

Evaluation No.	Week	Steps Due for Completion
1*	10/5–10/9	Business card designed and printed using silk screen
2*	10/26–10/30	Parts acquired, circuits designed, PC boards laid out on Mylar
3✝	11/23–11/25	PC boards fabricated and tested, packages designed, monitor program written
4	12/14–12/18	System electronically completed, packages fabricated, EPROMs programmed
5 (Final)	1/11–1/15	Project mechanically completed, documentation written up

* Completed.
✝ Nearing completion.

For the first evaluation, I had designed and printed a business card using the silk screen method of reproduction as was stated in the contract.

At the time of the second evaluation, I had acquired all the parts except for three 28-pin IC sockets, which were on order; the circuits had been designed; and the PC boards were designed and laid out on Mylar. I have since added my

2

name, the date, and "CSM" to all of my artwork in accordance with your instructions.

Since the third checkpoint is now approaching, I have been working on completing the scheduled steps. So far I have fabricated and drilled all five PC boards and have mounted most of the components on them. Also I have written a rough draft of the monitor program and have designed the basic outlines of the three packages. I expect to have the program and the package designs completed by the agreed upon date of 25 November.

At my present rate of production, I feel confident that I will complete my project on schedule. The system should be 100 percent functional before Christmas vacation (Evaluation 4) and be ready for the final comprehensive evaluation by 15 January 198_.

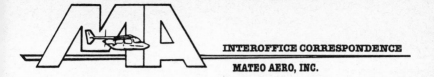

INTEROFFICE CORRESPONDENCE

MATEO AERO, INC.

TO: Chief Engineer, MA-202 Project   DATE: 21 April 198_
FROM: David Penney
SUBJECT: MA-202 Flap Configuration Report

1.0   INTRODUCTION

This is to inform you of my findings concerning
the proposed flap configurations for the MA-202. Of the
four proposed systems, the slotted Fowler flap mounted
on roller tracks within the wing offers the greatest
performance advantage and the most strength. Despite
the added weight and complexity of an internally
mounted system, I recommend it as the best overall.
(See Figure 1.)

Hinged Fowler

Slotted Fowler Flap

Plain

Plain Slotted

Figure 1   Proposed Flap System

1

2.0 DISCUSSION

Of the four proposed systems, I rejected the plain
flaps first because of their weak performance. The plain
slotted flaps were also rejected as not being effective
enough at the fully extended position. The two systems
remaining, then, were the externally hinged and the
internal track mounted slotted Fowlers. Figure 2 illus-
trates the performance advantage of slotted Fowler flaps
over the plain and plain slotted flap systems.

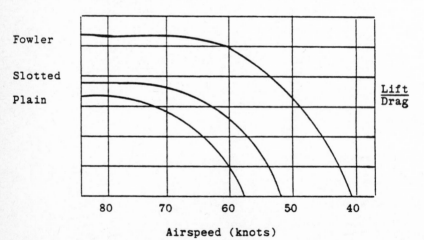

Figure 2   Flap Performance Comparison

2

The slotted Fowler flap offers the greatest range of operating speed by increasing the total lifting area as well as the curvature of the wing. Increasing the lifting area dramatically reduces the stalling speed for optimum short field takeoff and landing performance.

Research on the relative merits of the external hinge and the internal track mountings indicated a decided speed advantage without the added drag of external hinge assemblies. (See Figure 3.)

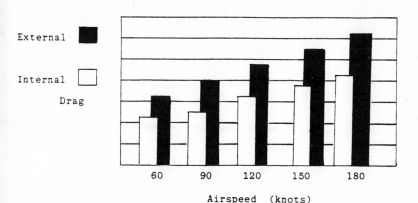

Figure 3   Flaps-up Drag Comparison

Since they are integral members of the wing structure, roller tracks also afford a stronger flap system.

3

The additional weight of the internal track system is estimated to be only five to seven pounds over the external hinges. This weight is more than offset by the added speed and fuel economy of the cleaner design. The complexity of the system can be kept to a minimum by using identical assemblies at all six wing-mounting stations.

3.0   CONCLUSION

Of the four proposed flap configurations for the MA-202, I find that slotted Fowler flaps offer markedly better performance than the plain and the plain slotted flaps. Of the two Fowler systems, the internal roller track mounting provides greater strength and less drag than the external hinge. I therefore recommend that this configuration be used on the MA-202.

THE SOCIAL AND ECONOMIC IMPLICATIONS
OF SUBSTITUTING
TELECOMMUNICATIONS FOR TRANSPORTATION

Submitted to
Anita Lehman
for
English 420 MWF
Writing for Industry
College of San Mateo
San Mateo, California
18 January 198_

by
George M. Meers

i

3033 La Selva B310
San Mateo, California 94403
4 January 198_

Mrs. Anita Lehman
Language Arts Division
College of San Mateo
San Mateo, California 94402

Dear Mrs. Lehman:

I have prepared the following report to complete the final
requirement for English 420, Writing for Industry. This
report is entitled The Social and Economic Implications of
Substituting Telecommunications for Transportation.

The intent of this report is to provide a general overview of
some of the economic and social implications of substituting
telecommunications for transportation. Three aspects of the
telecommunications-transportation tradeoff are discussed:
Part I considers the impact of telecommunications on
transportation, energy usage, and the environment; Part II
examines the relationship between telecommunications and
economic developments; Part III considers the impact of
telecommunications on human relations. This report
demonstrates the following conclusions: The difficulties
involved in substituting telecommunications for
transportation cannot be underestimated; as problems of
transportation congestion, energy shortages, and urban
growth continue to worsen, telecommunications will
achieve increasing importance and recognition.

Respectfully yours,

George Meers

George Meers

TABLE OF CONTENTS

LIST OF FIGURES

LIST OF TABLES

ABSTRACT

The intent of this report is to provide a general overview of some of the economic and social implications of substituting telecommunications for transportation. Three aspects of the telecommunications-transportation tradeoff are discussed: Part I considers the impact of telecommunications on transportation, energy usage, and the environment; Part II examines the relationship between telecommunications and economic developments; Part III considers the impact of telecommunications on human relations. This report demonstrates the following conclusions: The difficulties involved in substituting telecommunications for transportation cannot be underestimated; as problems of transportation congestion, energy shortages, and urban growth continue to worsen, telecommunications will achieve increasing importance and recognition.

THE SOCIAL AND ECONOMIC IMPLICATIONS
OF SUBSTITUTING TELECOMMUNICATIONS
FOR TRANSPORTATION

1.0 INTRODUCTION

The purpose of this report is to consider some of
the economic and social implications of substituting
telecommunications for transportation.

Telecommunications embraces a variety of submar-
kets: telephony, broadcast, cable television, educational
television, earth and satellite microwave radio links,
data communications, business and public safety communications, avionics, and telementry. (Careers:3)

Three aspects of the telecommunications-transportation tradeoff are discussed: Part I considers the impact
of telecommunications on transportation, energy usage,
and the environment. Part II examines the relationship
between communications and economic developments.
Part III considers the impact of telecommunications on
human relations.

The following conclusions are demonstrated: The
difficulties involved in substituting telecommunications

1

for transportation cannot be underestimated; as problems of transportation congestion, energy shortages, and urban growth continue to worsen, telecommunications will achieve increasing importance and recognition.

This report is in partial fulfillment of the requirements for English 420, Writing for Industry.

2.0 DISCUSSION

Part I of this report describes the impact of telecommunications on transportation, energy usage, and the environment. Part II shows the relationship between telecommunications and economic developments. Part III discusses the impact of telecommunications on human relations.

2.1 Part I: The Impact of Telecommunications on Transportation, Energy Usage, and the Environment

2.1.1 Impact of Telecommunications on Transportation

Studying 2,048 insurance company employees in Los Angeles, Jack Nilles and a team sponsored by the National Science Foundation found that each employee, on an average, traveled 21.4 miles a day to and from work.

2

These workers drove 12.4 million miles each year to get to work, using up nearly a half century's worth of hours to do so. (Nilles:78)

Table 1 shows the results of the cost estimates for the operation of a private automobile, using the average round-trip distance (21.4 miles) calculated for the employees. (Nilles:81)

TABLE 1   Direct Operating Costs of Private Auto Commuting

Cost Element	Average Annual Cost ($)
Depreciation	643
Financing	166
Maintenance	315
Gasoline, Oil	260
Insurance	198
Parking	450
Taxes	75
Total Costs	2,173

(Nilles:81)

At 1974 prices, the operating cost of private auto commuting was 22 cents per mile, or a total of $2,730,000 — an amount assumed indirectly by the company and its customers. The costs of commuting are indirectly passed on to the employer in the form of higher wages and to the consumer in higher prices. (Nilles:83)

3

Nilles found that the company was paying its downtown workers $520 a year more than the going rate in the dispersed locations, in effect "a subsidy of transportation costs." It was also providing parking spaces and other costly services made necessary by the centralized location. The elimination of this commuting cost could have permitted the company to add a substantial amount of profits. (Toffler:187)

The key question is this: When will the cost of installing and operating telecommunications equipment fall below the present cost of commuting? Whereas gasoline and other transport costs, including the costs of mass-transit alternatives to the auto, are soaring everywhere, the price of telecommunications is shrinking spectacularly. At some point the curves must cross. (Toffler:187)

> Satellites slash the cost of long-distance transmission, bringing it so near the zero mark per signal that engineers now speak of "distance-independent" communications. Computer power has multiplied exponentially, and prices have dropped so dramatically that engineers and investors alike are left gasping. With fiber optics and other new breakthrough technologies in the wings, it is clear that

4

still further cost reductions lie ahead—per unit of memory, per processing step, and per signal transmitted. (Toffler:187)

The additional cost of transferring employees to work centers near their homes would be for terminals plus communication lines to the central organization. Employees would walk or bicycle, rather than drive, to work centers near their homes, and they would pay at least part of the terminal costs in lieu of communicating expenses.

2.1.2   Impact of Telecommunications on Energy Usage

Alvin Toffler says that in 1975, had even as little as 12 to 14 percent of urban commuting been replaced by telecommuting, the United States would have saved approximately 75 million barrels of gasoline and would thereby have completely eliminated the need to import any gasoline from abroad. (Toffler:188)

The savings in energy and transportation costs can be dramatically illustrated by considering the decrease in round-trip mileage for the employees of the insurance company produced by the presence of up to 35 new work centers near their homes throughout the city. As shown in Figure 1, the average one-way mileage per employee would decrease from 10.7 to 3.1 miles. (Nilles:89)

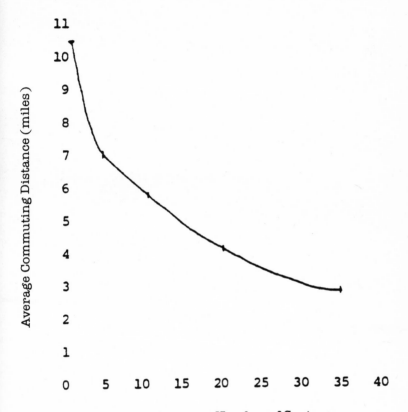

Figure 1   Average Commuting Distance vs. Number of Centers.   (Nilles:89)

The transfer of work, or any part of it, into work centers near the home could also lead to energy decentralization. Instead of requiring highly concentrated

6

amounts of energy in a few high-rise offices, and therefore requiring highly centralized energy generation, the
"electronic cottage" system would spread out energy
demand and make it easier to use solar, wind, and other
alternative energy technologies. (Toffler:191)

The estimated energy consumption for a car in a
typical Los Angeles round-trip commute of 22 miles is 50
kilowatt-hours, compared with only 2 kilowatt-hours for
computer and telephone lines. (See Figure 2.) (Electronics:38)

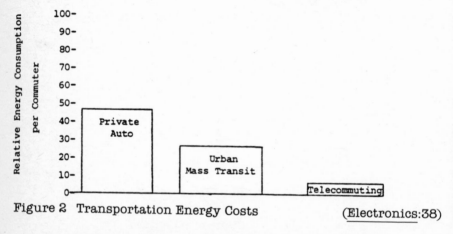

Figure 2   Transportation Energy Costs   (Electronics:38)

The Nilles team found that the average American
urban commuter uses the gasoline equivalent of 64.6 kilowatts of energy to get back and forth to work each day. (The
Los Angeles insurance employees burned 37.4 million
kilowatts a year in commuting.) By contrast, it takes

7

far less energy to move information. A typical computer terminal uses only 100 to 125 watts or fewer when it is in operation, and a phone line consumes only one watt or less while it is in use. (Toffler:188)

Making certain assumptions about how much communications equipment would be needed and how long it would operate, Nilles calculated that the relative advantage in energy consumption of telecommuting over commuting is at least 29 to 1 when the private automobile is used, 11 to 1 when normally loaded mass transit is used, and 12 to 1 for 100 percent utilized mass transit systems. (Toffler:188)

2.1.3 Impact of Telecommunications on the Environment

Telecommuting clearly reduces energy use where it substitutes for transportation. It also requires a different form of delivered energy than that required for most forms of transportation.

Both of these immediate results have consequences in environmental pollution. For example, urban automobile traffic makes up approximately 80 percent or more of the contribution to urban air pollution. For each 1 percent reduction in urban automobile traffic brought about by conversion to telecommuting, a reduction in urban air pollution of approximately 0.8 percent would result. (Toffler:191)

Furthermore the reduction may be even greater. Employees would walk or bicycle rather than drive to work centers near their homes. The energy demand would spread out and make it easier to use solar, wind, and other alternative energy technologies. This means smaller releases of highly concentrated pollutants that overload the environment at a few critical locations. (Toffler:191)

2.2   Part II. Relationship between Telecommunications and Economic Developments

Although the much-heralded office-of-the-future remains invisible, recent economic and social conditions have made its appearance more and more inevitable. Analysts of the office equipment industry claim that 22 percent of the total labor force, half the information industry, works in an office. Office workers' salaries account for up

to 50 percent of the total overhead costs of all U.S. corpora-
tions. (Stewart:15)

The Bureau of Labor Statistics says office support
workers earn about $300 billion a year, a figure that is ris-
ing at the rate of 6 to 8 percent a year. However, office
productivity has increased by only 4 percent in 10 years
compared with a 90 percent increase in industrial productivity over the same period, stimulated by automation.
While office employment and overhead costs have soared,
the price of office equipment has plummeted at an annual
rate of 10 percent, bringing increasingly sophisticated
computers into the reach of small businesses. (See Figure
3.) (Stewart:15)

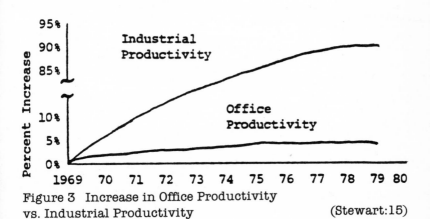

Figure 3   Increase in Office Productivity
vs. Industrial Productivity   (Stewart:15)

It has been estimated that the performance of computers has increased 10,000-fold in 15 years, whereas the price of "each unit of performance" has declined 100,000-fold since 1960. (Stewart:15)

Some businesses would shrink in the transfer to telecommuting and others would grow. (Toffler:191)

It is clear from the nature and purpose of the equipment that some people, mostly those with few office skills, will be put out of jobs; but it is equally evident that the telecommunications boost to productivity should create new, perhaps better jobs. (Stewart:16)

The electronics, computer, and communications industries would flourish. A whole new group of small-scale computer stores and information services would spring up. (Toffler:191)

2.3   Part III: The Impact of Telecommunications on Human Relations

The technology that makes progress possible was for a long time accepted without full consideration of its side effects. Recently, however, the notion that technological progress is synonymous with public benefit has been seriously questioned. At times the negative consequences of a new technique or device become so overwhelmingly evident that they cannot be ignored. (Wrightsman:432)

Hidden inside our advance to a new production system is a potential for social change so breathtaking in scope that few among us have been willing to face its meaning. (Toffler:181)

To suggest that millions of us may soon spend our time at home, instead of going out to an office or factory, is to unleash an immediate shower of objections. Alvin Toffler gives the following reasons for skepticism:

> People don't want to work at home, even if they could. Look at all the women struggling to get <u>out</u> of the home and into a job.
>
> How can you get any work done with kids running around?
>
> People won't be motivated unless there's a boss watching them.
>
> People need face-to-face contact with each other to develop the trust and confidence necessary to work together. (Toffler:181-82)

12

But at a different level, Toffler believes that work at home suggests a deepening of face-to-face and emotional relationships in both the home and the neighborhood and could mean greater community stability. (Toffler:192)

If employees can perform some or all of their work at home, they do not have to move every time they change jobs, as many have to do today. They can simply plug into a different computer. This means less forced mobility, less stress on the individual, fewer short-lived human relationships, and greater participation in community life. (Toffler:192)

Today when a family moves into a community, suspecting that it will be moving out again in a year or two, its members are reluctant to join neighborhood organizations, to make deep friendships, to engage in local politics, and to commit themselves to community life. The electronic community could help restore a sense of community association. (Toffler:192)

3.0   CONCLUSION

Substituting telecommunications for transportation has an impact on every aspect of American life: from transportation, energy usage, and the environment to economic developments and human relations.

Most high-technology nations are now having a transportation crisis, with mass-transit systems strained to the breaking point, roads and highways clogged, parking spaces rare, pollution a serious problem, strikes and breakdowns almost routine, and costs skyrocketing.

As these problems continue to worsen, telecommunications will achieve increasing importance and recognition. However the difficulties involved cannot be underestimated.

14

BIBLIOGRAPHY

"Communicating May Replace Commuting." Electronics (April 1974), 38.

Nilles, Jack. The Telecommunications Transportation Tradeoff. New York: John Wiley, 1976.

"Radio Frequency and Microwave Electronics." Careers in Engineering and Business. Palo Alto, Cal.: Hewlett-Packard Company, n.d.

Stewart, Jon. "Computer Shock." Saturday Review 54 (June 1979), 14-17.

Toffler, Alvin. The Third Wave. New York: William Morrow, 1980.

Wrightsman, Lawrence. Social Psychology. New York: Wadsworth, 1977.

APPENDIX C
Writing Guides and Checklist of Corrections

Writing Guides

1.0 OUTLINE THE REPORT.
  1.1 Define the problem. (What?)
  1.2 Do the research. (How?)
  1.3 Define the audience(s). (Who?)
  1.4 Formulate the rhetorical purpose. (Why?)
  1.5 Set the time line. (When?)

2.0 WRITE A ROUGH DRAFT.
  2.1 Start with the discussion section.
  2.2 Write the introduction.
  2.3 Write the summary or conclusion.
  2.4 Fill in the foreward segments.
  2.5 Fill in subheadings.
  2.6 Design figures and tables.

3.0 CHECK FINISHED COPY.
  3.1 Check for basic design.
  3.2 Check for attractiveness.
      3.2.1 Spacing
      3.2.2 Margins
      3.2.3 White Space
  3.3 Edit sentences.
      3.3.1 Clear
      3.3.2 Concise
      3.3.3 Forceful
      3.3.4 Correct
  3.4 Edit format.
  3.5 Check finished graphics.
  3.6 Proofread for elimination of all noise.

Warning   *Revise if necessary.*

Checklist of Corrections

	Excellent	Good	Fair	Poor

1.0 MECHANICS
  1.1 Abbreviations
  1.2 Capitalization
  1.3 Punctuation
  1.4 Spelling
  1.5 Correct usage
  1.6 Verbs
  1.7 Right words
  1.8 Simple words
  1.9 Exact words
  1.10 Footnotes
  1.11 Bibliography				

2.0 ATTRACTIVENESS
  2.1 Spacing
  2.2 Margins
  2.3 White space
  2.4 Headings and
      subheadings
  2.5 Numbering
  2.6 Graphics				

3.0 EDITING
  3.1 Accurate
  3.2 Complete
  3.3 Clear
  3.4 Concise
  3.5 Objective
  3.6 Correct				

4.0 EDITING (To eliminate all noise)				

Glossary

Access Tools Means by which one finds materials in the library: card catalog, indexes, reference librarian, audio-visual collection.

Analogy Correspondence in some respects, especially a function or position, between things otherwise dissimilar.

Communication The art of communicating thoughts, messages, or the like, as by speech, signals, or writing.

Decodes Receives message; converts from code into plain text.

Deductive Logic Inference by reasoning from the general to the specific.

Encodes Sends message.

Frame of Reference The framework into which ideas fit for the audience.

Initiated Audience No longer new at something; a technical audience that knows a great deal about the subject.

Lay Audience Knows little or nothing about the subject; uninitiated: needs to be given background material on subject.

Noise Interference of message; caused by incorrect spelling, punctuation, usage, and diction.

Objective To present factually, based on observable phenomena.

Plagiarism The act of stealing and using ideas or writings of another as one's own.

Source A person or place that supplies information.

Stimulus Anything causing or regarded as causing a response.

Symbols Printed or written signs used to represent a thought or an idea.

Technical Audience Knows a great deal about the subject; is initiated.

Technical Writing The art or skill of separating things and speculation from fact; organizing a logical presentation of evidence to support a convincing conclusion; and presenting findings in a clear, concise, and forceful piece of written prose.

Uninitiated Knows little or nothing about the subject; lay audience: needs to be given background material on subject.

Index